I talk to people on the radio every day who are up to their eyeballs in debt — too often the result of buying stuff they don't need just to live up to other people's expectations. *Altar Ego* reminds us that our true identity is found in Christ, not the stuff or people we keep piled up around us.

— DAVE RAMSEY, bestselling author and nationally syndicated radio host

To be who God wants us to be and to live as God wants us to live, we have to know who God says we are. This is a practical book to help you understand who you are, which will then transform all that you do.

— MARK DRISCOLL, founding pastor, Mars Hill Church

Altar Ego rattles loose the chains of complacency to help us believe with more faith and pray with more boldness. I love this book — the stories are captivating, the teaching inspiring, and the message one that will linger long after the last page is turned.

— LYSA TERKEURST, author, *Made to Crave* and *Unglued*

If you've ever struggled with your purpose in life and aren't sure where to turn next, *Altar Ego* is for you. So many times we search for our value outside of God's domain. We find our value in our accomplishments, our beauty, or our status. Altar your ego and discover what is possible with God on your side.

— JOHN C. MAXWELL, author, speaker, leadership expert

Craig Groeschel's accomplishments have earned him the credentials to share this message. But it's his posture of humility and spirit of selflessness that make him the greatest man of God I've ever known. *Altar Ego* will challenge you to lay aside your old life and take on the character of Christ.

— STEVEN FURTICK, lead pastor, Elevation Church; author, *Greater*

Most of us would like to change a few things about our lives, but Craig Groeschel helps us understand that we can't have a new life until we have a new identity in Christ. Once we let Jesus tell us who we are, it changes what we do.

— KYLE IDLEMAN, author, *Not a Fan*

If on more than one occasion your self-worth has been a function of your performance plus the opinion of others, this book is for you. *Altar Ego* will help you move from Edging God Out to Exalting God Only, and what a difference that will make in helping you become who you are meant to be.

— KEN BLANCHARD, coauthor, *The One Minute Manager* and *Lead Like Jesus*

Craig Groeschel told me years ago that the quickest way to forget what God says about me is to focus on what man says about me. Craig opens our eyes to the reality that we are not who others say we are but rather who God says we are, which really does unleash us to live a life that is filled with freedom and joy rather than guilt and worry.

— PERRY NOBLE, senior pastor, NewSpring Church; author, *Unleash*

Live the life God calls you to live. Craig Groeschel calls us to an honest, transformational relationship with Jesus Christ. It is all about him and who he made us to be for his glory. Read and apply the truths of this book to your life.

— DR. JAMES MACDONALD, senior pastor, Harvest Bible Chapel; author, *Vertical Church*

Craig Goeschel believes in you, and he's ready to hit you square between the eyes with the truth about who you really are. *Altar Ego* inspires and coaches us to sacrifice the unhealthy self-images we have so carefully crafted for ourselves so that we may unleash our true, God-given identities.

— TONY MORGAN, author, leadership coach, and consultant; TonyMorganLive.com

Craig Groeschel's *Altar Ego* is one of those rare books that God uses to flat out change your life. You are not who you think you are. You are who God says you are.

— KERRY SHOOK, founding pastor, Woodlands Church;
coauthor, *One Month to Live* and *Love at Last Sight*

Craig Groeschel always has a way of writing what I need to read, in the way I need to read it. In *Altar Ego*, Craig compels us to look inside and consider who we are, and who God is, so that we can live more grounded, spiritually healthy lives.

— JUD WILHITE, senior pastor, Central Christian Church; author, *Pursued*

None of us is who we want to be. When you look in the mirror, are you disappointed in the face staring back at you? If so, I hope you'll read this book. Stop worrying about the person you are not and begin to live in the reality of who God says you already are.

— GREG SURRATT, lead pastor, Seacoast Church; author, *Ir-Rev-Rend*

Craig Groeschel is open and authentic, sharing who he was and who he has become by the grace of God. You'll discover how to get past the labels that have defined you, and how to live with patience and integrity. If you desire to be all God intends for you to be, you need to read this book.

— DAVE FERGUSON, lead pastor, Community Christian Church; spiritual entrepreneur,
NewThing; author, *Exponential* and *Discover Your Mission Now*

I'm not sure why we're all so good at seeing pride, impatience, and self-aggrandizing duplicity in everyone else, but *Altar Ego* helped me redirect my gaze so I could see the truth about what's going on inside me. I'm not yet who I'm supposed to be, but *Altar Ego* filled me with hope that I can become who I am meant to be.

— MARK BEESON, founding pastor, Granger Community Church

Our culture is in a state of identity crisis. We often look in all the wrong places to derive our value. In *Altar Ego*, Craig Groeschel shows us who God says we are and why that truth is worth giving up everything and laying it all on the altar.

— ROBERT MORRIS, senior pastor, Gateway Church; author,
The Blessed Live, *From Dream to Destiny*, and *The God I Never Knew*

For anyone, like me, who fights to ground their identity on an unshakeable foundation and let go of the lust for approval, this book provides a solid centering, a scriptural perspective, and an honest voice.

— NANCY BEACH, lead coaching associate, SlingShotGroup

altar
ego

Other Books by Craig Groeschel

Becoming Who God Says You Are

altar ego

CRAIG GROESCHEL

ZONDERVAN®

ZONDERVAN.com/
AUTHORTRACKER
follow your favorite authors

We want to hear from you. Please send your comments about this book to us in care of zreview@zondervan.com. Thank you.

ZONDERVAN

Altar Ego
Copyright © 2013 by Craig Groeschel

This title is also available as a Zondervan ebook. Visit www.zondervan.com/ebooks.

This title is also available in a Zondervan audio edition. Visit www.zondervan.fm.

Requests for information should be addressed to:

Zondervan, *Grand Rapids, Michigan* 49530

This edition: ISBN 978-0-310-33383-8 (softcover)

Library of Congress Cataloging-in-Publication Data

Groeschel, Craig.
    Altar ego : becoming who God says you are / Craig Groeschel.
        p.   cm.
    ISBN 978-0-310-33371-5 (hardcover, jacketed)
    1. Identity (Psychology—Religious aspects—Christianity. I. Title.
BV4509.5.G696   2013
248.4—dc23   2012039760

Cover design: Jason Gabbert Design
Interior design: Katherine Lloyd, The DESK

Printed in the United States of America

19 20 21 22 PC/LSCC 24 23 22 21 20 19 18 17 16 15 14 13 12 11 10 9 8 7 6 5 4

contents

- PART THREE -
Sacrificing Self-Justification
for Passionate Obedience

to the reader

You are not yet who you are supposed to be.

The day I realized this truth was the day that changed my life.

I'll never forget the moment in college when I looked in the mirror and didn't like the person I saw looking back at me. As I glared into my hungover, depressed eyes on a cool, fall Saturday morning, I felt like I barely knew the guy trapped inside my reflection.

How did I end up here? Why did I do what I did last night? How did I become the person that I am?

Somehow I'd managed to fool a lot of people for a long time. To my teachers, I was a "good student." To my parents, I was a "good boy." To my college teammates, I was a "good athlete." To my party friends, I was a "good time."

For my whole life, I'd worked to protect my "good" reputation and be what everyone else wanted me to be. *What do you think of me? Do you like me? Am I good enough? Do I measure up?*

Do you ever ask questions like those? Do you work hard to please people, impress people, earn other people's love and respect? Do you worry about what people think as you labor to protect your reputation?

The problem is that your reputation is not who you really are.

Your reputation is who others think you are. Your character is who you really are.

On that unforgettable Saturday morning, I finally surrendered to the painful truth. Though my reputation was good, my character was not.

Leadership genius John Maxwell said, "The best definition of success is that those who know you the best, love and respect you the most." On that dark morning as I stared into the lifeless eyes reflected in the mirror, I realized that those who knew me the least, loved and respected me the most. Those who knew me best ... well, no one but me knew the real me. No one knew me better than I knew myself. And not only did I not love or respect myself, I despised myself.

Many had labeled me a good person, but nothing could be farther from the truth. I wasn't good. I was a liar, breaking promises and telling half-truths whenever it served my purposes. I was a thief, taking what didn't belong to me to improve my standard of living. I was a cheater, using cheat sheets on tests or betraying girlfriends when someone prettier came along. Truth be known, I was an all-around jerk. The only thing I was good at was fooling people.

You are not yet who you are supposed to be.

But I wasn't fooling God. And I wasn't fooling myself. And that's when it dawned on me.

You are not yet who you are supposed to be.

I was attempting to live *for* the approval of others rather than *from* the approval of God. My ego, that self-constructed identity I worked so hard to build, came from a twisted combination of my accomplishments and other people's opinions of me. If you liked me, I felt good. If you didn't, I felt bad. If I succeeded, won, or made the grade, I felt worth something. If I fell short, lost, or failed, I felt worthless. I loved myself just as conditionally as I assumed everyone else did. That Saturday morning, I realized I didn't have to continue this way. Someone did love me unconditionally. Enough to die for me.

If you've ever felt insecure, inadequate, or insufficient, this book is for you. Chances are good that you are like most of us. You attempt to draw worth or value from the wrong places. You're inclined to believe what others say about you over what God says about you. You say you believe one thing but privately live out of a double-standard set of beliefs. If you call yourself a Christian, you probably hope to live a life pleasing to God but often find yourself trying to please others or yourself.

If you can relate, I've got great news.

You are not yet who you are supposed to be.

Instead of living with an ego that is outward-driven and based on other people's approval, we're going to discover how to live with an altar ego. That's not a typo. I'm not talking about an alter ego like a superhero has to protect his real identity (Superman posing as Clark Kent). I'm talking about an ALTAR ego. Through God's Word, we'll learn to sacrifice our worldly self-image and let God replace it with his view of us. Rather than defining our worth by who we are in the opinions of others, we'll live from the truth of who we are in Christ. We'll place all of the false labels and selfish motives on the altar of God's truth and discover who we really are as his sons and daughters.

In this book, I'll show you specifically who God says you are.

You are his masterpiece, created perfectly in his image to do what he planned in advance for you to do. You are an overcomer, able to handle all of life's challenges by the inward strength of God through his Holy Spirit. You are an ambassador, sent by God from heaven to earth to represent him. You are not who others say you are. You are who God says you are.

As you discover your true identity in Christ, your altar ego will drive your actions, empowering you to live according to God's higher values, not according to the lower values of this world. Then, when you know who you are, you'll live with a deep confidence in God's calling. Rather than living a timid, halfhearted, shallow cultural Christianity, you'll boldly live in the confidence of the God who believes in you.

Are you willing to lay it all on the altar?

Almost twenty-five years ago, I stared into the mirror and couldn't stand the person that I saw looking back at me. At the time, I had no idea how those few moments would change the trajectory of my life. Even though I hated who I was, I discovered hope that I could become who I was meant to be. But for the first time in my life, I knew I couldn't do it on my own. I didn't need to try harder. I didn't need to turn over a new leaf. I didn't need to pick myself up by my bootstraps and give myself a pep talk. I needed to die to myself. And to let Christ live in me.

And in a series of events that only God could have orchestrated, that's what I did. Alone on a softball field less than a hundred yards from my solitary showdown in the mirror, I knelt before a holy God and then stood up as a very different person. Just outside the dugout on the third base side of the field, I unknowingly made the ground of well-worn grass into an altar. Kneeling before God, I left the old Craig Groeschel behind. From that moment on, I was never alone again. Christ was with me. Living in me. Loving me. Changing me.

The apostle Paul said, "I have been crucified with Christ and I no longer live, but Christ lives in me" (Gal. 2:20). That's what happened to me. By faith, my old life was gone, crucified with Christ. All the lies, all the cheating, all the stealing were forgiven and gone.

I no longer needed others to define who I was. Christ became my identity.

Although God transformed me spiritually in a moment, it has taken me years to grasp who I am as a child of God, and it's an ongoing process.

To learn who I am, I've had to learn who I am not.

You are not what others think about you.

You are not your past.

You are not what you did.

You are who God says you are.

If you are not a follower of Christ, my goal is to help you become one. If you are a Christian, then my prayer is that God will use this book to help you live with an altar ego. If you're ready to start becoming who you were meant to be, this book is for you.

PART ONE

Sacrificing Your False Self for Your Sacred Identity in Christ

overcoming the labels
that bind you

Don't rely too much on labels,
for too often they are fables.
— Charles H. Spurgeon

It's no secret that I've always been financially conservative — at least that's the way I've described myself. Others haven't been as kind in their descriptions of my careful spending habits. The refrain I've heard the most often is "Craig the Tightwad," which I find a bit extreme. I'm just more fiscally responsible than other people, I rationalize.

In my teens and college years, my financial selfishness didn't stand out that much. None of us had a lot of money to spend, so saving was pretty much out of the question. Sure, you might have been able to spot signs of my selfishness. Letting a buddy drive so I didn't have to pay for gas. Conveniently forgetting about a friend's birthday and the requisite gift. In college, some guys actually spread rumors that I'd break up with a girl before Valentine's Day to avoid giving her a present! For the record, if I ever did such a lousy thing, it wasn't more than once or twice.

When I was a young adult with a real job that paid a real salary (real low, but real nonetheless), my selfish tendencies became more obvious. When Amy and I married, my annual income was twelve thousand dollars a year. With the goal of becoming debt free, we held back on giving expensive presents to our friends and families. In the early years, our budget for Christmas was five dollars per person. When people made fun of us, we eventually caved and raised our budget to a liberal seven dollars per person. (Before you judge me, remember that seven dollars went a lot farther in 1991.)

The one habit that cemented my reputation, though, was recycling gifts. Anyone with the gift of penny-pinching has recycled a gift or two in their prime. I admit that I excelled and elevated regifting to an art form. Not only did I not want my kids to open the cellophane wrapping off some presents to ensure we could give those to another child as needed, but I regularly gave to others gift cards that I had received. The granddaddy of them all was when I actually got caught doing it. Sure, everyone suspected my crime, but no one could ever prove it, until the day I gave a Chili's gift card to Mike.

Mike was a painter who did some work on our home. Because Mike did a great job and wasn't a Christian, I wanted to be a good witness by offering him a tip for his work. But not wanting to drop any extra cash, I rummaged through my desk until I found a gift card to a Chili's restaurant. The little envelope it came in displayed the amount, and Mike seemed genuinely touched to receive a card with a twenty-five dollar balance. It was a win-win; Mike got rewarded and I didn't have to spend a cent.

The next night, Mike called me. "Craig!" he said. "Everyone said you're a tightwad, but this is ridiculous!" I could hear loud voices and the clatter of plates and cutlery in the background.

Oh no. My mind raced. *What did I do? How did he know?*

"I'm at Chili's with a friend and just tried to use the gift card you gave me," Mike said, his words coming out so fast I could barely understand him. "Our bill came to just over twenty bucks."

"Yes," I replied, as much of a question as a statement.

Mike didn't hold back as he unloaded on me. "The stupid gift card you gave me only had $2.43 credit on it!"

I had regifted a mostly used card. I guess I earned my not-so-coveted nickname, Craig the Tightwad.

READ THE LABELS

I'm not the only one to get saddled with identity baggage. You don't have to think long and hard to name people who've been labeled. There is Attila … the Hun. There is Conan … the Barbarian. Billy … the Kid. Buffy … the Vampire Slayer. And my childhood favorite, Winnie … the Pooh. Right or wrong, people are known for what they do. Tiger Woods was known for being the best golfer in the world. Unfortunately, because of his extracurricular activities, he has now picked up less favorable labels. Some people's names even become synonymous with their crimes or failures. No one wants to be a Benedict Arnold or a Doubting Thomas.

I've owned up to the negative nickname I earned, and I'm going to ask you to do the same. Even if you don't totally deserve what you've been called, it's important to acknowledge your label instead of pretending it doesn't exist or that it doesn't bother you. What's the label following your name?

Maybe you're Pam the People Pleaser, allowing others to walk all over you, rarely standing up for your rights or what you really want in life. Because of your passive nature, you've been labeled a doormat or a pushover. You're always concerned with what people think, worrying you've let them down, hurt their feelings, or disappointed them in some way. Perhaps people have labeled you as insecure, self-doubting, or apprehensive.

You might be more like Evan the Evasive, someone who postpones decision-making, always trying to keep your options open. Commitments make you feel tied down. So people say you're unreliable or uncommitted.

Or perhaps you're always getting your feelings hurt and people tiptoe around you because you're known to be overly sensitive.

Maybe you lose your cool more easily than most. You tend to say the first thing that pops into your mind. People have labeled you as angry and bitter, a hothead.

Or perhaps you have so much on your mind that you occasionally forget to return a call or a text. You often are late to meetings, if you make it at all. And you've been labeled irresponsible.

It might be that you've been the center of a few too many parties. You've lived on the wild side and had more than your share of late-night fun, and you've been labeled the party girl or the guy who is nothing more than a player.

Or maybe you don't feel like you excel at much of anything. You're not the worst, but you certainly aren't the best. And for most of your life, you've been called average. Mediocre.

SECRET IDENTITY

No matter what you have or haven't done, God's power is big enough to change you. There is no sin too great for God's grace. There is no habit too big for his healing. There is no label too strong for his love. Let me say it again, because I want you to believe this: God's power is bigger than your past.

And his power is rooted in his love for you. He knows who you really are no matter what others label you — or what you label yourself. What's true about you now doesn't have to be true about you later. The goal is not to reinvent yourself by striving to be some perfect person but to allow God to do an extreme makeover by uncovering your true self in his image, redeemed through Christ. What once was, no longer has to be. God can and will break the labels that have held you hostage.

> God's power is bigger than your past.

You were made for more than you've settled for. You know your life does not reflect who you really are deep down inside. You know there's more, and you're tired of settling for less, but you're just not sure how to move forward. It's time for you to learn who you really are and what you're capable of doing across eternity.

So many competing messages vie for our attention, trying to tell us who we are and what we should do, where we should shop and how we should vote, who we should cheer for and who we should condemn. But if we've committed to follow Jesus and have accepted the ultimate gift card of salvation, which carries an infinite balance over the charges of our sins, then there's only one source for knowing who we are and how we should live.

Overcoming labels will likely mean a radical shake-up of who you think you are. You may not even recognize yourself by the time you finish this book! My hope is that you'll discover greater harmony and peace in your life, a tighter alignment between your beliefs and your behavior. You will no longer be a collection of labels glued together by your acceptance of other people's perceptions of you. You will see the truth about who you are and how to live in the freedom of who you were meant to be.

HELLO, MY NAME IS . . .

When I became a Christian, I carried more labels than just Craig the Tightwad. Some people knew me as the frat boy who was the center of the party. Those on the outside of our party world often called me an arrogant jerk. The bottom line is, I felt like I had committed most of the sins a person could commit. As I shared in my opening letter to you, my self-image was lower than the belly of a worm crawling in the dirt. Not only did I dislike who I'd become; I outright hated myself.

That's why God's truth about who I am transformed my life and hope. Paul writes, "Anyone who belongs to Christ has become a *new person*. The old life is gone; a *new life has begun*!" (2 Cor. 5:17 NLT, emphasis mine). No matter what others have said or what you've believed about yourself, even if the negative labels are true, God can give you a new view of you.

He will start by giving you a new name. All through the Scriptures are multiple examples of God giving new names to replace old identities and to reflect new realities. Isaiah 62:2 says, "You will be called by a *new name* that the mouth of the LORD will bestow" (emphasis mine).

Can you imagine: the Lord of the universe bestowing upon you a new name to replace an old and hurtful label? God gave Abram and Sarai new names: Abraham and Sarah, meaning father and mother of many nations. Their new names pointed to God's promise of the blessings to come. God changed the name of Jacob, which meant trickster or deceiver, to Israel, the name of God's beloved chosen ones.

In the book of Judges, we read about a timid leader named Gideon. In our first impression, we see Gideon hiding in a winepress, afraid of the enemy, the Midianites. But when an angel of the Lord appears to Gideon, the angel calls him a "mighty man of valor." Gideon, empowered by God, grew into the true meaning of his name. God will do the same for you, but you must be willing to let go of the old name to grow into the fullness of your true identity.

Like Gideon and Jacob, so often we cling to the safety of a familiar, false identity rather than extend ourselves to grasp who we really are. People tell us we're shy, so we never allow ourselves to take risks to meet new people and become more social; we retreat into the safety of our refrain that "that's just who I am." Or they tell us we're funny and always expect us to crack a joke or deliver a witty punchline, never challenging us to use the intellect behind that humor for something more substantive.

I observed this phenomenon — and challenged it — when I first met my wife, Amy, more than twenty-two years ago, when she was a sophomore in college. Besides her love for God, I was impressed with her quick wit and sharp mind. So imagine my shock when one day Amy casually mentioned that she was just an average student. *Average student?* I remember thinking, *There is* nothing *average about this girl!* So I argued with assurance that she wasn't average at all.

Amy didn't budge on her self-proclamation of mediocrity. She dismissed my observation as the product of infatuation or flattery. When I tried to discern why she felt this way about herself, she explained that everyone — her parents, her teachers, her friends — always told her she was a middle-of-the-road student. For as long as she could remember, everyone agreed that she wasn't at the bottom of the class and never would find herself at the top. Her making mostly B's and a handful of C's only confirmed the label.

After several months of getting to know Amy even better, I was convinced that she believed a lie. With a burden that I felt came from God, I sat Amy down, looked her in the eye, and told her as boldly as I could, "Just because everyone else says something, and even believes it, doesn't make it true. You are not average. God made you very, very bright."

Amy's eyes almost glazed over as she instinctively brushed me off. Unfazed, I firmly but lovingly held both sides of her face and said, "Listen to me. I believe God wants you to hear this. Hear it as him speaking, not me. God did not make you average. You have greatness inside of you. It's time to act like it."

Her eyes teared and locked with mine. Something changed at that moment. I believe that instead of seeing herself as others saw her, Amy saw herself as God sees her. She started her next semester not as Amy the Average but with a new God-given name: Amy the Brilliant. If my story sounds a little cheesy or melodramatic, the results speak for themselves. For the first time ever, Amy made a 4.0 — all A's. With a new, God-given self-image, she never made anything lower than an A for the rest of her college studies.

THE BIG REVEAL

It wasn't long after this experience with Amy that God gave me a new name as well — one that I felt inadequate to own. Shortly after joining my church staff at the tender age of twenty-two, I passed a lady in our office. She smiled broadly and said, "Hi, Pastor Craig," and kept on walking. *Pastor Craig? Are you kidding me? I don't deserve to be called "Pastor" anything!*

Uncomfortable with this title, I found my boss, Nick, and told him that I wasn't ready to be called Pastor yet. I didn't know enough. Wasn't good enough. And still had way too much to learn. Pastor Nick burst out laughing, put his hand on my shoulder in a fatherly manner, and said, "Pastor Craig, I remember feeling just like you. Don't worry. You'll grow into your new name."

Those words helped change my life, and now the same is true of you. God is going to give you a new name; you may already know it.

You might not feel worthy of that name or understand how it applies to you. You may not feel deserving. Don't worry. God gave you that new name, and you will grow into it.

You might have done a lot of things wrong and you carry the guilt. Your new God-given name is Forgiven. Perhaps you've struggled with an ongoing sin or don't like something about yourself. Your new name is Transformed. You might live daily with a hurt from the past. You've been abused and don't know if you can ever overcome it. You have a new name. Your name is Healed.

> When God gives you a new name, by his Spirit and through his Son, you will grow into it.

It could be that you know you need to step it up and direct your family toward God's perfect will. Even though you don't feel ready, God calls you Spiritual Leader. You might have battled overeating or underexercising your whole life. Accept the new name Physically Fit. If you've ever felt like a failure as a mom, seek the God of all and own it when he calls you Great and Godly Mom.

When God gives you a new name, even if it feels like you can't fulfill it, don't worry. By his Spirit and through his Son, you will grow into it.

LIVING ON PURPOSE

Not only will "the Lord bestow upon you a new name" but your new name carries a new purpose. Again, God's Word is rich with examples. My favorite is Simon the fisherman because I relate to his inconsistencies, blunders, and well-intentioned failures. Like most of us, Simon didn't have the credentials expected of a spiritual hero. Many would have described him as unstable, unpredictable, and impulsive. But Jesus saw more in him than others saw.

And I can assure you that Jesus sees more in you as well.

Calling Simon to be his disciple, Jesus gave the fisherman a new name that carried a new purpose (see Matthew 16). After Jesus plays a round of spiritual *Jeopardy!* asking his followers who he really is, Peter lands the big money with the right answer. "You are the Messiah, the Son of the living God." In recognizing Jesus' true identity, Simon is stepping into a new name of his own. Jesus says, "Blessed are you, Simon son of Jonah, for this was not revealed to you by flesh and blood, but by my Father in heaven. And I tell you that *you are Peter*, and on this rock I will build my church, and the gates of Hades will not overcome it" (Matt. 16:17 – 18, emphasis mine). He is no longer Simon, but Peter. He will no longer cast nets for fish, but now he will be a fisher of men. God will use him to win people into God's kingdom.

Now, if you know anything at all about Peter, even after Jesus' declaration, Peter didn't always live up to his new name. (Like us, he still had to grow into it.) Numerous times Peter fell short of faithfulness. When the guards confronted Jesus near the Garden of Gethsemane, rather than responding as Jesus taught him, Peter resorted to violence and sliced off a soldier's ear. (I'm only guessing, but I'm pretty sure Peter was swinging for the head and missed.)

Peter's most infamous failure followed on the heels of his boldest declaration. When Jesus explained that many would fall away, Peter fought back, promising his allegiance. "Even if everyone else in the world falls away and leaves you," Peter declared with unbending boldness, "I will always be there for you and never let you down" (Mark 14:29, paraphrased). If you know the rest of the story, before the rooster crowed, Peter denied even knowing his Lord, not once, but *three* different times.

Even though Peter didn't initially live up to his new name and purpose, God helped him grow into it. His consistent shortcomings became his best teacher to learn about the grace and redemption of God through Christ. Since he was forgiven much, he knew how to preach on repentance and forgiveness. It's no wonder that God chose Peter to be the keynote speaker on the day of Pentecost as he unwaveringly told people to turn from their sins and turn to Christ.

Peter the Wishy Washy grew into his new name and his new purpose — Peter the Rock, called not to fish for fish but to fish for souls. History shows us that Peter died a martyr's death for his faith in Christ. Tradition says that his enemies planned to crucify him on a cross just like Jesus to mock his faith in Christ. But Peter begged them not to, explaining that he wasn't worthy to die in the same way as his Savior. Many Christians believe Peter was crucified upside down, displaying his love for Christ and his unwillingness to end his life in the same way as his Savior. Peter may have been born as quicksand, but he died a rock.

YOU'RE A GENIUS

When God helps you overcome a destructive label, he'll often do what he did through Peter. He will take one of your greatest weaknesses and turn it into one of your greatest strengths. It has been said that our weakness is our genius — our greatest struggle often yields the greatest opportunity for our growth. That's exactly what God did through me. My Lord transformed my heart and gave me a new name that carried a new purpose.

The closer I became to God, the more I believed God was calling me to a life of radical generosity. Over time, God changed my heart from that of a tightwad to that of one who lives to give. Though it started slowly, I grew into God's calling. Without question, I now know that one of my greatest purposes is to live well beneath my means and to give sacrificially to make a difference around the world.

This passion has overflowed into our church. Rather than selling products that our church produces, we strive to give away as much as we possibly can. It's hard for me to imagine, but more than one hundred thousand pastors and leaders downloaded from our church's website more than three million videos, messages, transcripts, and artwork pieces last year. We've been honored to give away YouVersion Bible apps by the millions every month. Our church is blessed to partner with hundreds of other churches who show my weekend teachings every week to their churches, all free of charge.

I may be a penny-pincher, but Amy and I are blessed to give away as much of our income as possible. Forgive me if this sounds boastful — that's not my intent — but we've been privileged to give away my book royalties, honorariums, and speaking income to bless ministries around the world. God took my greatest weakness (selfishness) and turned it into one of my favorite strengths (generosity). Craig the

Tightwad is no more. God calls me Craig the Generous, and I'm still growing into my new name and purpose.

I pray you experience God's grace as he removes a cruel label that you've owned. Perhaps you've gone through life struggling with a certain addiction. You've tried to kick it but always seemed to fail. Those around you know you as the Addict. But God will turn your weakness to strength. As the Overcomer, your new name, you will live for a higher purpose.

As God helps you defeat what once held you, you can do the same for others. Maybe you've been overweight most of your life and you've been labeled Fat. God can change your name to Fit. As you learn to eat right, exercise regularly, and tone your body, you can help others find the same freedom you've found.

Perhaps you're not good with money. You've lived with the name Broke or Struggling. Do not accept this as who you are! Have hope in God. You might start by studying Dave Ramsey's teachings (I know a guy with Dave's face tattooed on his arm) and over time, become financially free. Then God can use you to help others find the same freedom you know.

With your new name, God will always give you a new purpose.

REVISE THE FUTURE

Not only will God give you a new name and a new purpose, but by his grace and through his love, he will give you a new future. Jeremiah expresses the goodness of God's vision for us this way: " 'For I know the plans I have for you,' declares the LORD, 'plans to prosper you and not to harm you, plans to give you hope and a future'" (Jer. 29:11). While it's easy to believe the worst, God wants you to believe the best. He never promises a trouble-free life of leisure, but he does promise never to leave you and always to love you.

As you prayerfully banish labels from your life, you may have to alter your thinking about those labels' implication on your future. You might have heard, "You're always the bridesmaid and never the bride." This seemingly harmless phrase might rob you of the hope of a blessed marriage. Don't let it. Maybe others have said that you're one who simply can't commit. Or your divorce renders you useless in God's church. Brush away those lies like dandruff from your shoulders.

> When we know who we are and grow into our purpose, God revises the way we see our future.

If you've struggled in your marriage, you might be tempted to believe you will always struggle. Remember all things are possible with God. If you feel like an inadequate parent, believing you don't have what it takes to raise godly children, cast down the lie. When we know who we are and grow into our purpose, God revises the way we see our future.

My favorite example of God's redemption toward a better future is the story of a lady with a shady life. This woman is mentioned eight times in the Bible. Six of the eight times, she's identified with the darkness of her sultry profession as Rahab the Prostitute. Through her trade, Rahab had become a successful businesswoman running a profitable operation on the outskirts of Jericho. After giving her body to countless men, I'm certain she felt the pain that every person in such conditions eventually feels. Imagine her inward thoughts in dark, lonely, honest moments. *I'm used goods. No one will ever want me. After all I've done, I'll never find real love. Men want me for only one thing. If there is a God, he could never love me.*

If you know the amazing story, she encounters two of Israel's spies, who have come to check out her town. Rahab has heard numerous stories about the miracles of the God of Israel. Likely out of a desire to know more about their God, Rahab risks her life to hide the spies. If anyone in her town discovers and reports her crime, Rahab will immediately be executed for treason. Joshua 2:11 captures a beautiful picture of her desire for and curiosity about God: "When we heard of [all that God had done], our hearts melted in fear ... for the LORD your God is God in heaven above and on the earth below." Somewhere along the way, the God of Israel becomes the God of a prostitute.

Scripture makes it crystal clear that our grace-filled God gave the sin-stained woman a new hope and a new future. Though most would have believed Rahab would never marry well, she met a God-fearing man named Salmon, who loved her faithfully. And according to the first book of the New Testament, Rahab had a great, great, great, great, great-grandson named Jesus of Nazareth. That's right, from the lineage of a prostitute came the Savior of the world.

Isn't it time to peel off the many labels that cling to your reputation and uncover who you really are? It's not what you were that matters, but what you can become. And there is no name given to you that is more powerful than the name of Jesus. If God can bring Jesus into the world through the lineage of a prostitute, imagine what he wants to do through you.

you are God's masterpiece

When love and skill work together,
expect a masterpiece.

— John Ruskin

I'm going to let you in on a little secret about me: I've always battled deep feelings of insecurity. Most people seem to think I'm confident — even cocky, I've been told. Many people tell me I'm a natural leader, strong and even-keeled. But the truth is that I doubt myself every day. Or maybe that is no secret. Maybe it's always been really obvious, and I've just been kidding myself that people can't tell. (See what I mean?) Either way, my whole life I've been haunted by feelings that I'm not good enough, by worries that I might not measure up.

I had hoped that when I became a Christian that my insecurities would disappear. But that wasn't necessarily the case. It wasn't long after I committed my life to Christ that I had opportunities to speak publicly and to teach the Bible. At first, I declined every invitation, never feeling that I was good enough to teach the Word of God.

Finally, my pastor convinced me to give it a try. I was so nervous that I threw up in a garbage can right before taking the pulpit, a habit that continued for some time. For years, every time I spoke publicly, my face got blotchy, my neck flushed red, and I felt like I couldn't breathe. More than once, my wife, Amy, was worried there was something seriously wrong with me. But the only thing wrong was that I was freakishly nervous.

While my physical symptoms always faded as soon as I finished, my ego continued to suffer. After speaking or preaching, convinced I'd done a horrible job, I'd avoid going to the door. ("Going to the door" is what preachers do when they've done a good job preaching, so people can come by and say things to them like, "Nice sermon, Pastor!")

Probably after half a dozen efforts, I remember thinking, "Well, that message isn't going to win any awards, but I really think I did okay that time." So I decided to give myself a turn at the door to see what would happen. Afraid to hope, I longed to hear someone tell me, "Nice sermon, Pastor!" I would've been so encouraged to hear it just once.

The very first person to approach me was a very sweet, tiny lady in her late seventies. I smiled broadly, projecting as much charm as I could. She walked up and patted me on the shoulder, and I prepared to receive her generous words. Knowing what a kind, devoted, lifelong Christian she was, I expected to hear, "That was a fine sermon!"

Instead, she said, "Nice try. You know, if you keep practicing, you just might be a real preacher one day!"

I did my best to keep smiling, even though her words punctured my ego, driving my old insecurities deeper than ever before.

Maybe you can relate. No matter how hard you try, you feel like your best just isn't good enough. You try to please everyone in your life, and yet no one seems satisfied. You feel inadequate, inferior, and afraid of being found out.

You are not alone.

REALITY CHECK

Reality-TV shows thrive on showing us people who aren't good enough, people voted off the island, the ones told "you're fired!" and the ones with the least votes from home viewers. One of my favorites (to make fun of) is *The Bachelor*. Whenever I land on that show while channel surfing, there's inevitably a close-up of a young woman in a limousine, sobbing because she didn't get a rose — the Bachelor rejected her. She cries, "There must be something wrong with me! What's wrong with me?" Every time, I can't help thinking, "Um, let's see … You just spent thirty minutes with a guy you've never met before and you've decided he's the one true love of your life. And you're asking, 'What's wrong with me?' *Seriously*?"

I poke fun, but maybe you've experienced a similar kind of rejection. You felt abandoned by someone, or you didn't achieve what you wanted to. You thought you were going to do more, to be more, but it didn't happen. Your disappointment slowly bloomed into insecurity, an ongoing sense that you aren't enough. More and more, you may find yourself thinking, "There must be something wrong with me."

You know what? You're absolutely right; there is something wrong with you. With all of us. By ourselves, we'll never be enough. But once we surrender our lives to God, everything about us — including our mistakes and weaknesses — becomes the raw material for his masterpiece.

The first step — and it's the foundational step of your entire journey — is recognizing your need for a Savior. Be brutally honest. Whether or not you've committed yourself to Christ, maybe you don't like how things have turned out so far in your life. You had ideas, but they didn't pan out. You made plans, but they fell through. You had dreams, but now you've lost them.

"I know my life does not reflect the kind of person I really want to be. Something went wrong with it."

"I hoped to be more responsible with my money, but I got off track with my spending. Something went wrong with it."

"I planned to be a lot healthier at this age, but, well, something went wrong."

"I really thought I'd be married by now, but I'm losing hope that I'll ever marry."

"I believed I'd be a good person, generous and unselfish with my life, but life these days just costs too much."

"I honestly believed that God had all kinds of great things intended for me, but something went wrong along the way."

When something does go wrong, what's the best course of action? *To change your direction.* The word *repentance* means to stop going one direction (your own way) and turn toward the right direction (God's way). Your past may be a part of who you are, but it certainly doesn't have to define your future. Or if you feel stuck and unable to change directions and move toward God, think of this transformation another way. The Bible says that God is the Potter and we are his clay (Jer. 18:2 – 6).

And the best news for us is that God, the Potter, doesn't just throw away the clay, starting over from scratch with new clay. No, he uses the same clay, reshaping it into what he wanted it to be. If the choices you've been making have left you just a blob of dried out clay, God wants to remake you into his masterpiece, made new in Christ Jesus, equipped for the good works that God prepared in advance for you to do.

Without Christ as the center of your life, there's something terribly wrong with you. But with Christ, you are God's masterpiece. If you're serious about wanting to know who you really are, then you must realize your limitations as part of the process. It's critical that you understand the significance of your need.

PICTURE PERFECT

Even the greatest works of art in human history have flaws. A human artist strives to create work that captures the essence of her subject as close to perfection as possible. Regardless of the art form or medium, the artist attempting to reflect certain facets of his image or theme as precisely as possible will never reach perfection.

However, when we consider that we are God's work of art in progress, we discover that we are already his perfect workmanship in Christ Jesus; we don't have to try harder to earn perfection. In his letter to the Ephesians, Paul contrasts who we are without God and who we are with him. He writes, "God saved you by his grace when you believed. And you can't take credit for this; it is a gift from God. Salvation is not a reward for the good things we have done, so none of us can boast about it" (Eph. 2:8 – 9 NLT).

It doesn't matter how hard you try, how religious you act. You can't earn your way to salvation. You can't save yourself. Paul goes on to make his point about God's purpose in loving us enough to send his only Son to be sacrificed for us. "For we are God's *masterpiece*. He has created us anew in Christ Jesus, so we can do the good things he planned for us long ago" (Eph. 2:10 NLT, emphasis mine). There's a crucial distinction here about who we are and how we are to live. We are not saved *by* good works. We are saved *for* good works. Specifically, we're not saved *by* the good things that we have done, but we are saved *to do* good things on behalf of the one who saved us. And the good that we do is not for us to brag about. He saves us so we can make a difference in this world and bring glory to him.

If you're in Christ, it doesn't matter how you feel about yourself. Even if you think, "I'm not that good," or, "I'm not that talented," you need to understand this: You've been made new. You've been remade. You are God's masterpiece. But you're not just some painting that gets hung up on a wall where people can walk by and say, "Oh, that's a beautiful painting." No, you are God's masterpiece created to grow, serve, and glorify the Artist, who gives you life.

There's a bumper sticker I've seen on several cars that makes me chuckle. It reads, "God don't make no junk!" (Ironically, it seems like every time I see this bumper sticker, it's always on a car that's twenty years old and missing a fender.) But the truth is that when you're in Christ, God don't make no junk! You are his perfect work made for his glory-reflecting purpose.

The Greek word translated as "masterpiece" in Ephesians 2:10 is *poiema*. It means "a work made by God." Because we derive our English word *poem* from this word, I like to think of us as his beautiful poems. In Christ, your life should be a poetic statement of God's goodness. The Master Artisan designs our lives to interlock to create a big picture, a giant living tapestry, an enormous design interwoven with people's lives, an epic poem. Sometimes, from where we're standing, we might see where we fit. But if we can take a step back and look at it from his perspective, we can often glimpse the overall masterpiece, the perfect workmanship of God.

> The way God made you was not by chance or accident. You are divinely inspired.

The way God made you was not by chance or accident. You are divinely inspired, with his divine intention to guide you. Once you begin to grasp who you are — and whose you are — you begin to understand why you're here and what to do.

MY CUP RUNNETH OVER

In all of history, God decided that in this one little slice — this seventy years or eighty-two years or ninety-one years, whatever time you have on this earth — this was the single point ideally suited for you to serve him and bring him glory. Out of all of the nearly infinite possibilities, there was no better time for you to be born with your unique gifts, talents, skills, and personality. God knew you before you were, and he put you right where he wanted you.

Unfortunately, many of us don't believe we are masterpieces. We focus so much on our perceived deficiencies that we convince ourselves that God wouldn't use us, or perhaps even that he *couldn't*. Because we have not grasped who we are, we work hard to focus on all the things we are not. Consequently, we're not living out our true purpose; no wonder we're frustrated. If you don't know the purpose of something, all you can do is misuse it.

> If you don't know the purpose of something, all you can do is misuse it.

Allow me to illustrate with a memory from my childhood. When I was in the fourth grade, I had this next-door neighbor, Missy, who was in the fifth grade. Even though she was an older woman, Missy had a crush on me. (She was a cougar before cougars were cool.) One day, she came over to my house to hang out. At the time, my dad and I really loved playing baseball. We had just returned from a game, and we hadn't put away all of our equipment yet, so it was still in a heap in the corner of the kitchen.

There, in the mix of various sports gear, my dad had left sitting out a very important — even critical — element of his gear. There's no way to put this delicately, I'm afraid. This particular device is specially designed, for a man, to cover and protect his very personal equipment. It's called a cup.

Now, if you're not familiar with male sports equipment (as Missy was not), you could be forgiven for wondering, "You mean like a cup that you drink out of?"

But that would be mistaking its function because of its name. It's actually a concave, triangular piece of thick plastic, usually padded a little on the side that goes against your body. This protective device cups the most vulnerable area of a man's body during sports, preventing injury and excruciating pain.

What happened was like in one of those movies when a child picks up a weapon or an explosive device, and all the adults begin running toward the child in slow motion, screaming silently as the catastrophe occurs.

Missy picked up my dad's cup.

We were all scrambling to reach her, crying out, "No, no, no! Put that down! Don't touch it! You're a girl! That's … not … right! Nooooooo!"

Missy looked up, apparently oblivious to our protests, and asked innocently, "Hey, what's this?

"Oh!" she exclaimed, smiling broadly. "It's an oxygen mask, right?"

She cupped it over her mouth and began breathing deeply, in and out.

At the time, I would have said we were all really grossed out. But I'm older now, and I know more words, so I think words such as *aghast* or *appalled* are more accurate.

I'm going to say it again: if you don't know the purpose of something, all you can do is misuse it.

If you don't know the purpose of your life, all you can do is misuse it. Whether through waste or selfishness, your ignorance will have you squandering the masterpiece of God that is you. Life with no purpose is time without meaning. When you don't know the purpose of your life, everything you do is just an experiment. You just try on one thing after another, always hoping that the next shiny thing that catches your attention will finally be *the one thing* that makes a difference. There's a problem with this approach (several, actually). If you don't know the purpose of a thing, you can't ask the thing what it's for. You can't pick up an athletic cup and say to it, "What are you for?" So the next thing you know, you might be pressing it against your face, trying to breathe through it. A far better strategy would be to ask the one who made it. You are God's masterpiece. Wouldn't it make sense to ask God what you should do with your life?

If you've been living according to some grand plan, whether to accumulate as many things as you can or to be as famous as possible or even to achieve world domination, let me tell you: you're thinking way too small. Your purpose is far beyond this life. It's actually eternal. Everything that God made, he designed to reflect his glory back to himself. And every one of us — each of his works of art — does this in our own specific way.

ENOUGH IS ENOUGH

As God's masterpiece, called to do his good works in a way that is all your own, you have everything you need to fulfill your purpose. The fact that God made you in this way tells us something else very important about your life. You have everything you need to do everything God wants you to do.

Don't take my word for it. Let's look at what Scripture says: "[God's] divine power has given us everything we need for a godly life through our knowledge of him who called us by his own glory and goodness" (2 Peter 1:3). First, notice that according to this verse, a godly life doesn't happen under our own power; it happens by God's divine power. Next, make sure you realize what God's divine power has given us. *Every* thing. Every *thing*. *Everything*. In case you're wondering, the Greek word translated as "everything" in this verse, *pas* (pronounced PAHS), means "everything." It also means "each, every, any, all, the whole, all things." You know ... "everything."

God is never caught off guard. He doesn't ask people to do something, then realize later that they weren't equipped to do it and say, "Whoops! My bad! I don't know what I was thinking. You don't have what you need to do that!"

When God called Moses to lead the Hebrew people out of their slavery to the Egyptians, Moses didn't believe he was good enough to do it (see Exodus 4). He didn't believe he was a masterpiece. He argued with God, "I'm not a good speaker. I can't do this!" And you'll remember from the story that God slapped his forehead and answered, "Oh, my me, Moses! You're right. I guess I just *thought* you could do it, but you're obviously not good enough!"

Of course, God never did that. When God calls you, he equips you with everything you need to do everything he wants you to do. I believe that this common scarcity mentality that some people have boils down to something I call "masterpiece envy." That's when people compare themselves to other people, making excuses for themselves:

"Well, I'm not a good speaker like Steven."

"Dave's really good with money, but I never have been."

"I sure wish I had Beth's confidence."

Scripture tells us that when we compare ourselves with each other, we are not wise (2 Cor. 10:12). Instead, we should be focusing on the unique ways God created us. We say, "I *wish* I could do that!" Instead, we should be discovering and acknowledging those things that we *can* do. What are the things you can do that other people can't? God has given you everything you need to do everything that he wants you to do.

When I speak God's Word, I can sense God's Spirit empowering me. God created me to share his truth. Of course, there are far more things that I *cannot* do:

I can't sing. When I try to sing, dogs howl and birds migrate. I'm pretty sure what I do doesn't even qualify as a joyful noise.

I'm color blind. Not only can I not paint or draw; I honestly don't even understand art. My wife, Amy, looks at a painting and sees minute details, losing herself in a canvas, oohing and ahing and saying things like, "How beautiful! God has gifted this person with extraordinary talent." I look at the same thing and say, "What ... you mean these wavy line things?"

I can't fix anything. I may be the only person I know who's gifted at breaking things that are already broken. You may have heard that old saying, "If it ain't broke, don't let Groeschel anywhere near it!" I'm so bad at fixing things that I can't even fix a sandwich.

But those things don't matter to me. Because I wasn't created to sing. I wasn't created to paint. I wasn't created to fix broken appliances. And what difference does that make in God's blueprint for my life? Other people were created to do those things, and it's my great joy to let them live out the talents God made them for.

Stop focusing on the things you *can't* do. Turn your attention to the things you *can* do. You are the masterpiece of God, created for the Master's purpose. Don't flip through the catalog of things you aren't, wishing you could order a few nice things for yourself. Instead, look at the sales brochure for you. Start meditating on the truth about you: "I am the masterpiece of God. I'm a new creation in Christ Jesus. I already have everything I need to do everything God wants me to do."

GOOD TO GRACE

Even as you're reading these words on this very page, God is shaping you. Paul tells us, "And we know that in all things God works for the good of those who love him, who have been called according to his purpose" (Rom. 8:28). In how many things? *All* things. Does all things include the good things? Yes! Does all things include the bad things? Yes! Does all things include things you're glad happened? Yes. Does all things include things you wish had never happened? Yes.

In *all things*, God works for the good.

So here's another question: does this verse apply to everybody? Actually, no. This verse makes it really clear, God works in all things to bring about good "for those who love him," and for those "who have been called according to his purpose."

If you are following Christ, you are the masterpiece, created for the Master's purpose. He is the Potter. You are the clay. He's working all things for the good of those who love him and are called according to his purpose. Once you begin to look at your life from his perspective, you'll start to find tremendous confidence. You can trust him. You can trust that he is the sovereign, good God. From there, it's a natural extension to step into his will and discover his purpose for you.

Scripture offers us example after example of people who loved God and were called according to his purpose, yet struggled through serious challenges (many for years!) before they ever saw his vision fulfilled for their lives. One of my favorites is a young boy named Joseph who dared to believe that he was God's masterpiece when circumstances constantly told him otherwise.

It started when God gave him dreams and visions, which he shared with his family: "I'm going to be a great leader one day!" He was the youngest, and all of his brothers disagreed with Joseph. So they did what any good brothers would do to help out their little brother: they faked his death and sold him into slavery. (Boy, I'm glad I only have a little sister!)

Do you think Joseph thought, "Hey, perfect! Slavery! This is the next logical step toward fulfilling my leadership vision." Of course not. But the Potter was shaping his clay into his masterpiece. Even in his distress, Joseph used the gifts that God had given him. He was so talented and faithful to his new owner, Potiphar, that he was promoted (Genesis 39). Then one day, Potiphar's wife looked at him and said, "You look good! I want some of that!" (Okay, I'm paraphrasing.) She made moves on him, but he resisted and ran away, so she falsely accused him of attacking her, which got him sent straight to prison.

I just reread this story and couldn't find anywhere where it says, "And Joseph was really happy that God allowed him to be sent to prison to continue to prepare him for his future." No, the closest thing it says is that "the Lord was with him." The Potter was humming along, busily shaping his clay.

Through an unusual series of events, after Joseph interpreted some dreams, he was freed from prison and promoted again, this time to become second in charge over all of Egypt. In Joseph's new position, God used Joseph to help prepare for a massive famine. Years later, when his brothers came for grain, they found themselves standing before him, the very brother they had sold into slavery and assumed was dead. When Joseph revealed to them who he was, they knew they were as good as dead.

Instead, he looked on them with compassion, and through his tears he said, "No. I'm your brother! I forgive you! What you meant for evil, God has used for good." Everything that had happened to Joseph up until that moment had shaped him, forming him into the powerful man he now was. The path to his greatness and best use led him through years of difficulty and injustice. He couldn't see it until the very end, but he remained faithful and continued using his gifts. And God used all of that adversity for good.

Maybe you can relate to Joseph. Maybe you're going through some tough times, and you're thinking, "Man, I wish this wasn't happening." It can be painful, I know. You don't understand why things are happening the way they are. You wish things were different. You've even prayed that God would change your circumstances. But the truth is, according to Scripture, if you are in Christ, if you love him, if you're living for his purpose, he's working in *all things* to bring about good. Our God is good like that.

Who are you? Think about everything that characterizes your life and defines you. Think about the experiences you've had, the decisions you've made, all the people you've loved, the trophies you've won, and all those times you've blown it. Are you good enough? By yourself, no.

But he is.

He's more than enough. His grace is more than enough for you. You are who you are — you are *where* you are — because he set you on this path, plotted this course for you. And right now, in this moment, as you're reading the words on this page, it's because God put them in front of you for you. (And you know it's true, don't you?) Without Christ, there's something wrong with you. But with Christ, you are God's masterpiece. You are created for his purpose, and you have all you need to do all that God wants you to do. And nothing will be wasted; God will use everything in your life to fulfill his vision for you.

> When you know who you are, you will know what to do.

When you know who you are, you will know what to do.

chapter 3

you are
an overcomer

When everything seems to be going against you,
remember that the airplane takes off
against the wind, not with it.

— Henry Ford

Have you ever had "one of those days"? You know, no matter what you do, nothing goes the way it's supposed to go. Several years ago, I had one of those days on steroids. I awoke extra early in my hotel room in Chicago to prepare for one of the biggest meetings of my life. In less than two hours, I was supposed to pick up the host at his hotel and drive him to "the big meeting."

Normally, I wouldn't order room service, but I thought it would save time plus allow me to eat before I got dressed, so I wouldn't have to worry about getting eggs on my tie. I had requested a 7:00 a.m. delivery, and by a quarter after, my carefully thought-out schedule was about to fall apart. Minutes ticked by and still no eggs.

In my best try-to-stay-cool attitude, I called the restaurant. A polite lady apologized and explained that they'd misplaced my order. The bad news: my eggs would be even later. The good news: they would be free.

Normally, I'd be jumping for joy to save $14.95 (plus tax, tip, and delivery), but I didn't have time. I would have to get dressed first and then eat before rushing out the door, a risky move before my big meeting, but necessary to keep moving.

Looking into the bathroom mirror, I tied the perfect Windsor knot to complement my carefully ironed white dress shirt. The moment I got everything in place, someone knocked on the door. Breakfast had arrived.

Noticing that I'd lost the time cushion I'd worked so hard to include, I scarfed down the eggs. When I grabbed the glass of orange juice for one final swig, I accidentally spilled some in my lap.

Arggghhhh! I didn't cuss, but I was definitely tempted as I tried to rub out the juice with a warm washcloth.

Stress set in. Big meeting. Spilled juice. Tight on time. Not good.

I grabbed my briefcase and rushed to the parking lot. The freezing Chicago air blasted me in the face. *I should have brought an overcoat.*

Low on gas from two days of driving my micro-economy rental car, I sped to the nearest gas station to fill up and drive through the car wash. Because I was unfamiliar with the car, I drove up to the gas pump with it facing the wrong way. Instead of losing more time, I simply stepped out into the subzero temperature and pulled the gas nozzle across my car. Shaking from the cold, I tried to get the gas to come out. Again and again I squeezed the handle. When nothing came out, I pulled the nozzle out to look at it and squeezed again. This time gasoline squirted out all over my suit.

You gotta be kidding me! Thankfully, still no cussing, but I was even closer than the first time.

Smelling like two parts gas, one part OJ, I put five bucks in my tank and drove to the car wash.

The moment the water sprayed around my car and instantly froze, I knew I'd made a huge mistake. Within seconds, my Ford Escort turned into a popsicle.

Unable to see through the solid layer of ice on the windshield, I slowly drove out of the car wash. When I tried to open the door, I discovered that it was frozen shut. Panic set in. I couldn't see to drive forward. And I couldn't open the door to get out.

Suddenly fighting for my life, I moved over to the passenger's seat, reached for the door handle on the driver's side, and kicked as hard as I could. After a dozen attempts, I shattered the ice and opened the door.

Running dangerously low on time, I ran inside the convenience store and purchased a cheap ice scraper. Within minutes, I scraped away a ten-by-ten-inch square that gave me partial visibility. I prayed as I drove across Chicago to pick up my host, realizing that the passenger's-side door would be frozen shut as well. When I got to his hotel, only a few minutes late, I had the valet call for him while I chiseled away at the ice on the car door.

He came out to meet me, and I shook his hand, well aware that I looked like a stray dog that had frozen in an alley somewhere. Trying to act normal, I made small talk as he climbed into the passenger's seat.

With both of us in the front of the car, our breath fogged up the window and my limited visibility became virtually no visibility. That's when I drove head on into the median and blew out the front tires.

All of us have challenging days, and when they snowball (or iceball, in this case), it can seem like there's no end in sight. Perhaps you've had one recently. Unfortunately, a lot of people have more than tough days; they have crushing weeks, months, or years, with adversaries much greater than spilled juice and flat tires, such as divorce, unemployment, cancer, addictions, and the loss of loved ones.

If you feel like David staring at Goliath, I've got great news for you. You are not small. You are not outmatched. You are not defeated.

By the power of Christ, you can overcome.

FIGHT TO THE FINISH

Life has a way of hitting us hard. My pastor used to say you're either coming out of a tough season, in the middle of a tough season, or heading into a tough season. Perhaps you can relate. Maybe you just have too much to do and you feel overwhelmed. Or maybe it's worse for you. Maybe it feels like everything is too much, like life is just kind of happening to you. Maybe you're facing some kind of obstacle, an opponent, a challenge you just don't believe you can overcome.

Your personal Goliath could be anything. It could be something temporary, like my schedule. It could be a season, looking for another job or going through an illness. Or maybe it's even ongoing, like struggling with your weight, facing depression, or battling a stubborn addiction. Maybe it's emotional or spiritual, like someone hurt you and you know you need to forgive them, but you just haven't been able to bring yourself to do it.

Whatever you're facing, even if it's too big for you, if you have committed your life to Christ and have God's Spirit within you, then I have really good news: by God's power, you are an overcomer.

Scripture is filled with numerous examples of people just like you and me who overcame everything from whales' bellies to lions' dens, from Egyptian armies to stormy weather. The passage

> **By God's power, you are an overcomer.**

I love the most is from Paul's letter to the Christian church in Rome. He begins by asking rhetorical questions — "If God is for us, who can be against us?" — which he then proceeds to answer.

Paul continues, "He who did not spare his own Son, but gave him up for us all — how will he not also, along with him, graciously give us all things?" His point is so urgent and all-consuming that he drives it home by asking, "Who shall separate us from the love of Christ? Shall trouble or hardship or persecution or famine or nakedness or danger or sword?" (Rom. 8:32, 35).

Even today, some two thousand years later, these seven obstacles remain just as relevant for us as they were for Paul's readers. Let's look at these briefly, one by one, and reflect on how you may be encountering them in your life right now.

Trouble or hardship. Troubles and hardships certainly seem to transcend time. You might be facing some kind of trouble or hardship right now. It could be ongoing migraine headaches. It could be a crumbling marriage. It could be that one of your kids has been getting bullied at school. Those are troubles. They're hardships. So I'll put Paul's question to you: will those things separate you from the love of Christ?

Persecution. Maybe you're in school and others harass you for bringing your Bible with you. Or maybe you're single and have committed to save your virginity for marriage and it feels like everybody's making fun of you. You might be a businessperson, and you walked away from a very profitable deal because you'd have to compromise your integrity to close it. Maybe other people around you — your partners, even your spouse — don't understand and they're angry with you. Will that persecution separate you from the love of Christ?

Famine or nakedness. Chances are pretty good that if you had the money to buy this book, you're probably not going hungry. Certainly, there are millions of people in our world today for whom hunger is a sobering reality. Even if you're not naked or in famine, what about financial challenges? Does it ever feel like there's more month left than money? Do you ever worry about where the money for groceries is going to come from? Or for school clothes for the kids? Or how you're going to juggle car payments, school loan payments, and credit card payments?

Danger or sword. I know many people who live in countries where, if they were to go public with their faith in Christ, their lives would be in jeopardy. In the country where I live, that type of danger is not very common. But danger or sword could very well represent some other kind of physical danger to you. Maybe you've been in an abusive relationship, and the other person has threatened to harm you or someone you love — or maybe they even have already. Maybe you heard a bad report from your doctor, and the next few months are promising pain and peril. Paul asks, "Who shall separate us from the love of Christ? Shall trouble or hardship or persecution or famine or nakedness or danger or sword?"

We are more than conquerors.

Well, that all depends. Who do you think you are? Because when you know who you are, you'll know what to do. Who are you in Christ? Paul emphatically answers his own question: "No, in all these things *we are more than conquerors* through him who loved us" (v. 37, emphasis mine).

HYPER POWERS

In all of these various obstacles and challenges, we are more than conquerors. It's important that we acknowledge that this promise is fulfilled not through our own power but through the power of the risen Christ, who loves us. If you follow Christ, you are more than a conqueror, more than an overcomer.

The little Greek word that appears in various translations as "conqueror," "winner," "victor," or "overcomer" is the word *nikao*, which means "to win, to be victorious, or to gain a surpassing victory." But that's not the word used in this passage. The word Paul uses here is *hupernikao*, which means "to vanquish beyond recognition, to gain a decisive victory, to conquer exceedingly." With Christ, you are *hupernikao*! You are not going to just eke out some tiny, insignificant victory. No, you're going to demolish the opposition.

Your victory is the God kind of victory, where God vanquishes the opposition beyond recognition. Imagine Pharaoh's army chasing the Israelites to the edge of the desert, and God parting the Red Sea in front of them. The Israelites cross on dry land, and the entire Egyptian army follows them in. Then God withdraws his hand, and *whooooosh!* all of them are washed away. It's total victory!

Consider Gideon, God's reluctant warrior, in my butchered paraphrase from Judges 6 – 8. God tells Gideon, "I want you to take on the Midianites."

But Gideon responds, "I just can't do it! I'm too scared!"

"No! You're a mighty man of valor," God tells him. "You might not believe it yet, but you are!"

"But I have only thirty-two thousand men!" Gideon whines.

God shoots back, "You're right. That's no good. That's way too many for me to get the glory!"

So God pares those down to just three hundred and tells Gideon, "Now, you guys take your weapons and your pitchers. Light some torches, cover them up, blow your horns, and break your pitchers."

Gideon says, "Uh … I'm sure you don't know what you're talking about, but we'll do it. You are God and everything … I guess."

Then when Gideon's men work God's plan, the whole Midianite army turns on itself in confusion and wipes itself out. And that is *hupernikao.* That is who you are in Christ! You're more than victorious. You are *hupernikao.*

Now, what I'm not saying is that you'll never have a hard time in life. The Bible doesn't say that at all. Jesus makes it clear that "in this world you will have trouble." But think about this for a minute: to be an overcomer, you have to have something to overcome. And Jesus continues, "But take heart! I have overcome the world" (John 16:33).

EXTRAORDINARY

If you follow Christ, then you have access to his power. You might not think of yourself as extraordinary, but the fact is, there's no such thing as an ordinary Christian. You are a Spirit-filled overcomer. But don't take my word for it. Let's look again in God's Word.

Revelation 12:11 says, "They triumphed over him by the blood of the Lamb and by the word of their testimony." According to this chapter of the Bible, the "they" are those who follow Christ (us!). The "him" is our enemy, the devil, Satan. "The Lamb" is Jesus, the resurrected King of Kings and Lord of Lords.

Here's what I want you, an overcomer, to see. Two things allowed these believers to triumph over their enemy: the blood of the Lamb and the words of their testimony. Let's look at each one of these:

> *You are an overcomer by the blood of the Lamb.* If you've never heard of this before, you might think it sounds gross. But actually, it's great news for you. In the Old Testament, to receive forgiveness for sins, people offered animals (often a lamb) to God as a sacrifice. The shedding of the precious and valuable blood — the source of life — is what cleansed them of their sin.
>
> Then Jesus presented himself one time — the most precious blood of all — as a final sacrifice for the forgiveness

of our sins. Jesus became the ultimate Lamb of God. His blood alone has the power to forgive us once and for all. Because he chose to shed his blood for us, we have overcome the sin that held us hostage.

You are an overcomer by the words of your testimony. Your testimony is simply your story, but it's also more than that. If you witness something happening, and you're called in to court as a "witness" to "testify" — or in other words, to give your testimony about what happened — you know exactly what that means. That means you're an eyewitness to the events and can help establish the truth for all of the people who weren't there. The judge has you swear that you'll tell the whole truth about everything you saw. And your testimony isn't about you, either. It's about events that you happened to be present for, to see, to experience, to observe.

So your testimony is your story with God. Who were you before you gave your life to Christ? Who are you now because of Christ? The transformation of your life by his power is your story, the words of your testimony.

If you follow Jesus, then that same Spirit of God that empowered David to defeat a giant named Goliath, that same Spirit who later raised Christ from the dead, lives inside of you. That's what makes you what you are. Just like David, you are an overcomer. Not by your own strength, but by the blood of the Lamb and by the words of your testimony.

To be all that God intends for you to be, to fulfill all of the chapters that God is writing in your story, you need to understand this, to internalize it, to feel it. We're not talking about someday in the future. This is now. This isn't what you're going to become. This isn't, "Once I can get my life together ..." This isn't, "Once I can beat this stubborn addiction of mine ..." This is who God says you already are.

Maybe there's a giant who has everyone around you paralyzed. Maybe no one else thinks you can beat it. (Maybe even you don't think you can.) But I'm telling you, by the power of the risen Christ, you can. You are *hupernikao*. More than a conqueror.

You ... are ... an ... overcomer.

VICTIM NO MORE

Tragically, many people have this faithless, wishy-washy mindset, which causes them to lose the battle in their minds before they ever fight it in the world. But that's not you. Who are you? If you truly follow Christ, then you're already more than a conqueror. Faith-filled attitudes lead to faith-filled actions. Godly beliefs lead to godly behavior. The battle starts in your mind. Have you ever found yourself having these kinds of thoughts?

"Everybody else always gets the breaks. Nothing ever goes right for me."
"My marriage stinks. It's never going to get any better, because my spouse is always going to be a jerk."
"Ugh! I'm just never going to get married. Everybody calls

it Valentine's Day; what they should call it is Singles'
Awareness Day. Table for one, please!"

"I'm always going to be overweight. I might as well just give up
and keep eating."

"Nothing I've tried works; I'm never going to get over this
addiction."

"I don't care what anybody says, I'm never going to be able to
forgive them for what they did to me."

Do you know what kind of thoughts those are? Victim talk. And
are you a victim? Well, are you? If you're a Christian, then you are
not a victim. Through the power of the risen Christ, you are a victor.
So put your foot down. Draw a line in the sand. Stop that self-defeat-
ing mindset in its tracks, once and for all. You know who you are in
Christ. You are *hupernikao*! You vanquish the enemy. You're not just
an overcomer; you're more than an overcomer.

When negative thoughts bombard my mind, I quote 2 Corinthians 10:3 – 5: "Though we live in the world, we do not wage war as the
world does. The weapons we fight with are not the weapons of the
world. On the contrary, they have divine power to demolish strongholds. We demolish arguments and every pretension that sets itself up
against the knowledge of God, and we take captive every thought to
make it obedient to Christ."

Demolish. That's a great word, isn't it? That's not just squeak-
ing by. That's not just barely beating those thoughts. That means
total, absolute, complete destruction. That means that you take that
negativity, you lift it up over your head, you bring it crashing to the
ground, and you crush it into rubble. Demolish it!

OFF THE WALL

If I sound passionate, it's because I am. Almost everything worthwhile I'm doing today is a result of God helping me to overcome a challenge, a problem, opposition, or my own doubts.

Back when I began serving in ministry (many years ago), I worked for five years at a terrific church. My first year, the board decided I should be fired. My first year! I didn't even make it to my one-year anniversary! It's only because my senior pastor, Nick, stood up for me and convinced them to give me another chance that I'm still in ministry today.

Not only did the church board have their reservations about me, but so did my denominational leaders. After their one-year screening process for ordination, a group of men called me in to give me their conclusions: "Craig, we are not sure you're called to ministry. Your ideas are just too ... Well, let's just say we're not sure you'd make a good pastor."

Rather than ordaining me, they agreed to observe me. I continued to do everything they asked, including completing my master of divinity degree. I jumped through every hoop they wanted me to. During that time, I served in full-time ministry, was a full-time student, and a full-time new dad. And then, finally, after everything, they agreed to license me for ministry.

After graduating from seminary, I asked humbly, "May I start a church now?"

Their answer: "Well, um ... no."

No.

I was crushed. "What can I do? I'll do anything you say. Can I *ever* start a church?"

Their answer: "Nothing. And sorry, son. Still no."

No.

I came up against wall after wall after wall. If I didn't know who I was, I could have said, "Well, I guess God doesn't want me to do anything. Hey, I know: maybe I could go into sales!"

But for as long as I can remember, I've always believed that even if I come up to a wall that's in my way, with my God, we'll go over it, we'll go under it, or we'll put our heads down and go through it. Why? Because Psalm 18:29 says, "In [God's] strength I can crush an army; with my God I can scale any wall" (NLT).

There it is again: *hupernikao.* Crush your enemy. Vanquish him. Scale any wall? That's Spider-Man, baby! No wall is going to stop us from doing what God wants us to do. Are you a victim? No! In Christ, you are an overcomer. You have the power to overcome all of the temptations and hurdles this world throws at you. Fight ... with a conquering attitude.

LESS THAN A MIRACLE

The second way we fight as overcomers is with supernatural weapons. You'll recall from 2 Corinthians 10:3 – 5 that we are well equipped to do spiritual battle. Our weapons aren't the same kind of weapons people of this world use; our weapons have divine power. The word *power* here is a translation of the Greek word *dynatos.* If it seems familiar to you, perhaps it's because it's where we get our word *dynamite.* Our weapons have the explosive power of God. They have the divine power to demolish strongholds.

If you're a Christian, you need to know who you are and what you have. Check Ephesians 6:10 – 20 for the inventory of what's in your supernatural arsenal. Buckle your utility belt of truth around your waist, and fasten your breastplate of righteousness in place. Get on your boots with readiness from the gospel of peace. Pick up your shield of faith to deflect and put out the fiery darts of your enemy. Finally, pull on your helmet of salvation, and pick up your sword of the Spirit, which is the living Word of God.

Then plunge headlong into the fight. Vanquish the enemy. Fight with the spiritual weapons God has equipped us with. Thinking about it this way may seem goofy to you, but once you experience it, you'll never discount it again.

Recently I was reminded that truly nothing is impossible with God, no matter how bleak the situation may appear. Erica, one of our church staff members, saw her thirty-eight-year-old husband, Jeff, suffer a massive heart attack. By the time the ambulance arrived at their house (after only a few minutes), he was unconscious and unresponsive. Uncertain how long he'd been without a heartbeat, the paramedics went right to work, shocking him repeatedly and continuing CPR. They loaded him up and raced him to a local heart hospital, where highly skilled professionals determined that he was clinically dead.

Still, because they had been able to get his heart going more than once — only to then see it stop again a few minutes later — they refused to give up on him, shocking him again and again until they could get him hooked up to proper life-support systems. According to their official records, by the time they reached that point, he had not breathed on his own or had an unassisted heartbeat for more than an hour and a half.

As soon as we heard what had happened, Amy and I rushed to the hospital to check on Erica. I was devastated about this whole situation. Jeff was not overweight, didn't smoke, and did nothing that would have put his heart at risk. It just didn't seem fair.

Before we headed to Jeff's room in the ICU, we visited with a few ER staff to get the whole story, and especially to hear about his chances. It was grim. One nurse told me, "Well, he won't be going home. Not to his earthly home, anyway."

I frowned. "What about with a miracle?"

He sighed. "Well, let's say he miraculously regains consciousness. That doesn't really gain us anything. Because he's showing zero brain activity. We can keep his body 'alive' with the machines, but his brain was without oxygen for a *looooong* time. Your brain just can't handle that."

Amy and I took a deep breath together, agreed on a strategy, steeled ourselves, and went in. Our plan was just to make sure Erica knew how much we loved her, what her family means to us, and that we were going to be there for her, that we were going to help her get through this, no matter what happened.

First, we prayed for Erica, pretty much the standard pastoral stuff: "comfort," "peace," "God's presence" — those kinds of things. And there was Jeff, just a couple of feet from where we were sitting, surrounded by tubes and wires and drips, everything poked into him, surgical tape strapped all over his body. His breathing was audible and regular, a machine rhythmically forcing his chest to expand and contract. Another machine beeped out each heartbeat as it gave it to him. I realized what a machine the human body actually is, sophisticated, intricate, magnificent in its complexity. And it occurred to me: Who made it? And who did this man belong to?

My frustration turned to inspiration, from inspiration to anticipation, from anticipation to hope. It was slowly dawning on my lightning-fast mind: "Our God can do this. He can heal Jeff. He can!" But that was not what we'd been asking for. So I decided to do something pretty radical. I decided I'd ask God to heal Jeff. I put my hand on Jeff's body — which I found out later you're not supposed to do — and I said out loud, in faith, "God, I believe you can do this!"

I found out later that I was late in getting to this party. Hundreds of people were already praying for Jeff's full and miraculous recovery. Over the next few days, Erica started hearing from all over the world that powerful Christians were praying for them. Less than a month later, Erica left that hospital with Jeff walking next to her, under his own power.

He couldn't live. He did. If he lived, he was going to be brain dead. He isn't. If he had any brain capacity at all, it would be significantly diminished. It isn't. He remembers everything from before he blacked out. He can walk and talk and think just like he could before. He can't dance, but he couldn't dance before anyway.

I am a witness to what God did in Jeff and Erica's lives. Jeff is an overcomer. By the blood of the Lamb and by the words of his own testimony.

Jeff is an overcomer. And if you follow Christ, you are too. If someone tells you:

"I'm really sorry. Your situation is hopeless."

"There's just no chance."

"No one has ever."

Then here's what you should be hearing in their words:

"Get your armor on!"

"Our God is able!"

"Greater is he that is in you than he that is in the world!"

"Fight!"

It's time to fight. With supernatural weapons, it's on. It's a rumble in the jungle, a battle royale. Fight. Fight. Fight. Fight. Fight. Get this: Don't you give up. You're not a victim. You're an overcomer. Fight!

Don't just fight like a man; fight like a man of God. Fight like the warrior princess that you are. Go with confidence into the very throne room of your Father, the King of Kings, and ask him respectfully to intervene on your behalf. Tell him boldly, "I believe you can, Lord! This world sees no hope, but you are my hope."

When you accept the fact that your true identity includes being an overcomer, you will never settle for less than a miracle.

you are God's
ambassador

We are therefore Christ's ambassadors,
as though God were making his appeal through us.
We implore you on Christ's behalf: Be reconciled to God.

— 2 Corinthians 5:20

Several years ago, we had our church's central offices in this little, rundown industrial park, and my office overlooked a parking lot. One afternoon, as I was looking out over my beautiful asphalt view, I saw at least fifty cars rush into the lot and come to an abrupt halt. Within moments, dozens and dozens of high school students piled out of the cars, gathered in a big circle, and then these two guys, both muscular jocks, stepped into the circle and took their shirts off. They wasted no time squaring off and trading blows. Everybody brought out their phones and cameras and started videoing as these two guys just blasted each other. Instinctively, I got really excited, and I ran through our office yelling, "Fight! Fight! Fight!"

A friend and fellow pastor, Robert Wall, got just as excited as I was. Rushing from our building, we couldn't wait to get outside and join the other spectators in watching these two kids beat the crud out of each other. Fueled by adrenaline and more testosterone than two middle-aged pastors had felt in some time, we were yelling, "Hit him! Yeah! Hit him!"

About sixty seconds into the fight, Robert and I glanced at each other as it finally dawned on us. We were grown-ups, we were Christians, and we were pastors. We were not supposed to be cheering for two seventeen-year-olds to whale on each other like contestants at a World Cage Fighting title bout. We were supposed to be stopping the fight and restoring order. And so, finally, we both got closer and, still admiring a nice punch or a good move, shouted, "Break it up! Come on, guys, break it up!"

Someone in the crowd saw us and screamed, "It's Pastor Craig! Run!" And everybody rushed to their cars and peeled out of the parking lot as quickly as possible. I suddenly felt the full weight of my authority; talk about being a peacemaker!

Now before you judge me for watching too much ultimate fighting on late-night cable, I think this little incident clearly illustrates a problem that many of us seem to battle: spiritual amnesia. For the briefest of moments, I forgot who I was and flashed back to my own schoolyard brawls. I lost sight of being a minister of the gospel, let alone a responsible adult. For those couple of minutes, I forgot who I was and what I should do. Then it came back to me: I'm a grown-up. I'm a Christian. I'm a pastor. I don't cheer for kids who are hurting each other; I try to break up fights.

BLINDED BY THE LIGHT

As I've shared with you, the problem many of us have as Christians is that we don't understand our new identity in Christ. And because we don't know who we are, we often don't know what to do. So far, we've discussed overcoming old labels — the misperceptions, judgments, and definitions imposed on us by others and by our critical egos. We've looked at what it means to be God's masterpiece, a work of art in progress with God transforming us into the image of his Son. Last chapter we focused on all the power we have as overcomers in the fullness of our identities in Christ. Things that look impossible from our point of view are effortless in God's eternal perspective.

Now it's time to think about what it means to represent, reflect, and resonate with the character of God as we live as ambassadors of Christ. This may be the most crucial facet of our new identity because it translates directly into how we act. When we internalize our faith, and it goes from this intellectual knowledge to a true heart-belief, everything changes.

Perhaps there's no more dramatic example of such a transformation than the one we see in the apostle Paul. As you may know, Paul wrote about two-thirds of the New Testament. But if you know his past, you know he was the least likely guy to be called a man of God. He began his career as the number one persecutor of the Christian church. He killed the followers of Jesus and seemed to relish their persecution.

But Saul, as he was known then, encounters Jesus, the risen Christ, while traveling on the road to Damascus, and the brightness of his glory blinds Saul. God tells him to go to a nearby city, where another Christian named Ananias will help him. But when Saul shows up on his doorstep, Ananias thinks, "No way! This dude will kill me! I know his story." But God intervenes and tells Ananias, "This man is different now. He is my chosen instrument to carry my name before the Gentiles. He is my ambassador to the rest of the world. I've chosen and appointed him to represent heaven on earth for those who are not Jewish" (see Acts 9:15).

To go with his new identity, God changes Saul's name to Paul and sends him to share the incredible news of Christ around the known world. So when Paul writes, "Therefore, if anyone is in Christ, he is a new creation; the old has gone, the new has come!" (2 Cor. 5:17 NIV 1984), he knows what he's talking about. He went from being a ruthless bounty hunter and murderer to being a man in love with God who was willing to endure unlimited persecution. He had to lay down his old identity, his ego-driven role of persecutor, to embrace his new identity as an altar-ego-driven man of God.

The same is true for you and me. If you are in Christ, if you are a Christian, if you've turned from your sins and met the risen Christ, then you are a new creation. The old, the filth, the junk, the sin, the guilt, the shame — it's all gone. All of your sins have been forgiven; you're a new creation. The problem, though, is that some Christians don't understand what it means to be a new creation. It's like a caterpillar becoming a new creation, the butterfly. But imagine if the butterfly broke out of his cocoon and just crawled around like a caterpillar. Some of us have been transformed to fly and yet continue to crawl around on the ground, missing our true calling and divine potential.

DOUBLE STANDARDS

So are you spiritually soaring or are you crawling right now? If you feel like you're still on the ground, then it's time you realized that God wants you to fly. You're not just another average, run-of-the-mill Christian barely making it. No, if you're a Christian, then there is nothing regular about you. You must understand that you are filled with the same Spirit that raised Christ from the grave, and there's nothing ordinary about that!

You have access to the very throne of God; that's not regular! You have the authority to use the name that is above every name, the name of Jesus Christ. There is nothing regular about you. And — you know it — when you know who you are, you'll know what to do. If you know who you are in Christ, then you'll know how to represent him wherever you go.

> If you know who you are in Christ, then you'll know how to represent him wherever you go.

This is true for all Christians, not just select people who are called into full-time vocational ministry. Let me tell you something that just drives me crazy. I go nuts when people try to hold me to a higher standard simply because I'm a pastor. Every area of my life gets scrutinized and held to this higher level of accountability: the way I spend my money, the way I spend my time, the way I talk to people, the movies that I watch, the way I raise my kids, the words that I say.

Recently, I experienced this simply because of something I posted on my Facebook page. When Amy turned forty, I wrote, "Happy forti-eth birthday, Amy! I love you with all my heart. And you are way better than two twenty-year-olds!" And a lot of people whined and complained and scolded me with, "Oh, a man of God shouldn't say things like that."

In my defense, please consider a couple of important points. Number one, it's true — my wife is better than two twenty-year-olds. Number two: it's funny. (At least it is if you have a sense of humor.) Okay, maybe I'm pushing the edge here; I'll give you that. But please don't tell me I went over the edge just because I'm a pastor. Sure, I'll be judged more strictly for what I teach. (See James 3:1.) But when it comes to how we live, all Christians should be held to the same standard. I'm not saying I should be brought down to a lower standard. No, I'm saying that if you're a Christian, *you* are Christ's ambassador and you too should be at a higher standard in everything that you do.

It's funny, at big banquets or dinners, or at holidays, when it's time to eat, someone will say, "Pastor Craig, would you bless the meal?" Now, I'm certainly happy to pray and to pray with other believers. But in these situations, I love to turn the tables and say, "I'd be glad to, but why don't you pray a blessing on our meal?" Almost every time I say this, the other person says, "Oh no, no, no! You're the pastor and I'm just a regular Christian." I love seeing people squirm. And so I tell them that I may have more practice praying out loud but that I'm no better at praying than they are. All Christians are called to be Christ's representatives here on earth.

Paul describes our mission this way: "[God] has committed to us the message of reconciliation" (2 Cor. 5:19). Notice that it doesn't say that he has committed elders or deacons or pastors or missionaries.

No, God has committed to us — all of us — his message of reconciliation through Christ.

If we consider the meaning of reconciliation in the context of the original Greek language, it means "to restore to the divine." Basically, it means to help people be made right with God. It's to take that which is broken, as we are separated from God by our sin, and to help others know who Christ is so they can be whole and made right with God. God has committed to those who are Christians the message of reconciliation. Paul concludes, "We are therefore Christ's ambassadors" (v. 20).

You are an ambassador. God has committed to you the message of reconciliation as though he were making his appeal through you.

This makes sense as we consider the job description of an ambassador. Traditionally, an ambassador serves as the highest-ranking diplomat sent as a representative from one country to another. For example, if I became the ambassador of the United States to Egypt, then I would be the highest-ranking diplomat sent to represent the US government to Egypt. The same is true for you. You are the highest-ranking diplomat sent by God, from heaven to earth, to share with those around you the truth of your homeland. Earth is not your home. The Bible says that you are an alien here. This is not your final destination. You're sent to represent the King from the kingdom that sent you. You represent the King of Kings and the Lord of Lords.

HALL PASS

As Christ's ambassador, you were not elected by people, but you were chosen and appointed by God. It doesn't matter what anybody else thinks. Jesus said, "You did not choose me, but I chose you." He said, "I appointed you to go and bear fruit — fruit that will last. You do not belong to this world; this isn't your home. You're from heaven; you're an ambassador." (See John 15:16 – 19.) He has chosen us.

You may say, "But I don't feel good enough; I'm not (whatever) enough." But our excuses have nothing to do with what qualifies us: God has chosen and equipped us, regardless of how we may feel about it. It's a little bit like being in grade school and having the teacher choose you to deliver a message to the principal's office. She wouldn't necessarily pick the student who made all A's or is the best athlete or is the most popular. She would just select someone she trusted, someone reliable, someone she believed in.

You'd pass your friends in the hall and they'd ask what you were doing. And you'd say, "I've been chosen and appointed by the teacher to go and do something special. I'm not the best, but baby, I've got a hall pass!" No matter what others may say to you, the good news is that God has chosen and appointed you for his special mission. He's given us the authority to serve him in ways that we could never accomplish on our own right where we are.

Your mission might be to represent God to the people you work with. You are his chosen instrument to illustrate who he is and what he's like to your coworkers or others in your office. It could be to the people in your family. You're God's chosen instrument to represent him as an ambassador to your family. It could be to the people on your Thursday night basketball team. Or the women in your book club. Or the guys in your fraternity. You're not just good enough; God says you are the best at representing him where he has placed you.

I have to remember this truth every time I speak before a crowd. Most weekends, I deliver a message to tens of thousands of people at all of our different campuses, network churches, and online. But I never see more than several hundred in one location. If I saw them all at once, it would freak me out! The first time I ever spoke in front of tens of thousands of people in a huge stadium, I looked around and almost lost more than just my voice! It was so intimidating. So I closed my eyes and said to myself, "I am God's chosen instrument to carry his message today." And I could step in with that authority. I'm not the best, I'm not a Bible scholar, but God has chosen and appointed me, and I take confidence in this truth.

You're not just good enough; God says you are the best at representing him where he has placed you.

You can do the same thing. You may say, "But I can't speak in public." It doesn't matter, because it's not about your speaking ability or the size of the crowd. I sometimes get more nervous one-on-one than I do one-on-hundreds of people. I recall a recent conversation with a good friend of mine. We had been close since college and now this guy made some really bad decisions, sinful decisions that would adversely affect his life and others. And I was the only guy who knew about this, which meant I had to go and confront him.

This wasn't Pastor Craig the church leader, or a Christian church member to another member. This was buddy to buddy, friend to friend, man to man. There was nothing in me that was excited about the impending conversation, but somehow I knew that I was there to represent God's presence in the midst of the mess my friend was making. So before the meeting, I just said, "Okay, God, obviously I am your chosen instrument for this situation," and this allowed me to have confidence despite the hard things that I needed to say.

Maybe God's calling you to represent him to teens, youth, the next generation. You may think that you're too old to be cool or too young to be a mentor, but if God places you in a situation, then you know he'll empower you. Maybe he wants you to lead a small group even though you've never led anything before. Or maybe he's given you a really difficult boss to work for, and it's clear that you may be the only glimpse of Christ this person ever sees.

It could be just that you're good at repairing cars and you're driving down the road and there's a young woman and her car is broken down. You become God's chosen instrument to help her fix her car. You think, "Okay, I can do this. I can serve in the name of Jesus Christ and represent him by serving her in this way."

As Christ's ambassador you never represent yourself; you always represent God. If I'm the ambassador to Egypt from the United States, I'm not there to promote my own agenda, my own values, my own ideas; I represent the government that has sent me. You represent the government of the kingdom of God. You represent the King of Kings and the Lord of Lords. It's never about you. Jesus was the ultimate ambassador, and he said what we too should say: "For I have come down from heaven not to do my will but to do the will of him who sent me" (John 6:38).

MAKE YOU SWEAT

When we serve as God's ambassadors, we are always on duty, maybe when we least expect it. For almost twenty years, I've been working out regularly at the gym with the same workout partner. One day, we miscommunicated and my buddy didn't show up. So it was a rare day because I was there by myself. At the end of my workouts, I usually treat myself to a sauna. (That way, no matter what, I always look really sweaty and people say, "Wow, you worked out hard." Little trick of the trade.) So I went in there as usual, only it was probably the first time in years that I was alone.

After a few moments, this other guy walked in and there was just the two of us. From his facial expression, I could tell that he was in pain, more than just pain from a hard workout. Even though he was in his late twenties or early thirties, he looked burdened beyond his years. His body language conveyed resignation and defeat. So I tried to start a conversation with him, grateful that he didn't know who I was or what I did, just as I didn't know who he was. I said, "Hey, man, it's obvious you're having a bad day, and I don't want to pry, but if you want to talk, I'll listen."

Within a few minutes, he opened up. He didn't go into the details, but evidently he had done something he regretted. Somehow he had betrayed his wife and they got into a big fight. So he decided his marriage was over and had moved out the day before. He broke down and said, "I'll never forget my three-year-old daughter, as I'm backing down the driveway, crying, 'Daddy, don't leave us, don't leave us!'"

And he had driven away and now felt like his world was shattered beyond repair.

At that moment, I realized my workout partner wasn't supposed to be here today so that I would be here alone with this guy. Trying not to sound like a preacher, I said as plainly as possible, "I don't want to sound overly religious or anything like that, and I don't know where you stand with God, but I want to tell you that I believe God sent me here today to tell you that you need to go home and get on your knees, apologize, and start again." He looked back soberly as I continued, "And I believe God wants you to be the daddy to that little girl and the husband to your wife. And I'm just saying this because I believe God wants me to tell you this message."

The guy choked up and said, "I want you to know that I'm not a religious guy at all, but I think you're right. I believe God sent you here to tell me to go home."

I wasn't trying to force him to pray and accept Christ there in the sauna. I wasn't in there inviting him to church. I just listened to God's Spirit and relayed the message I heard. That's what an ambassador does. When you're aware of your diplomatic status, you will find all kinds of opportunities to represent God.

> You don't have to know what to say or what to do; just listen to the one who sent you.

You don't have to know what to say or what to do; just listen to the one who sent you. It's his authority that authorizes us to speak on his behalf and not our own. Take Paul; over and over again he said, "I'm not an eloquent speaker, I just preach by the power of the gospel. I'm the least of the apostles. I just do this in the authority that's been given to me by Christ." And he wasn't afraid of what people thought or how they might misunderstand. He explained, "I may seem to be boasting too much about the authority given to us by the Lord. But our authority builds you up; it doesn't tear you down. So I will not be ashamed of using my authority" (2 Cor. 10:8 NLT).

We must not be ashamed of using the same authority. It's not our power; it's the power of the one who appointed us. If I stand in the middle of a street with traffic everywhere and you're driving toward me and I tell you to stop, what could you do to me? You could run me over, right? Because I'm just some goofy guy standing there talking. I've got no authority to tell you to do that.

If, on the other hand, I have a badge that says I'm a police officer and I tell you to stop, you know what you'd better do. I have the whole government standing behind me, and it's not me telling you to stop; it's the law. And so, as a Christian, I come not in my own authority, but in the authority of the Lord Jesus Christ.

It's like if one of my kids comes in. Little Sam, he's twelve, came in yesterday and said, "Dad, Stephen's chasing me and he won't stop!" I said, "Well, tell him to leave you alone." Sam said, "But he won't listen to me!" I looked down at Sam and said, "You tell him that Dad said so!"

So Sam went into the other room and relayed my message. All of a sudden there was a little more authority in his message because he was sent on a mission as an ambassador of the king of kings of the household, who sent him to set things straight. When we know our source, we draw on the strength of that source.

First-century believers understood that their power was in Jesus and not in themselves, that they had that authority to use his name. They would say, "Sick person, I've got no power to heal you, but in the name of Jesus Christ, be healed," and sick people were healed. They would say, "Demon-possessed person, I've got no power over demons, but in the name of Jesus Christ, come out!" Or, and this is freaky, they would say, "Dead person, you're dead; in the name of Jesus come back to life."

Even crazier is that the New Testament says that we, as believers, can do even greater things. (See John 14:12.) Why? Because there's no such thing as a regular Christian. You are an ambassador of Christ. You were not elected by people, but you were chosen and appointed by God to represent heaven on earth.

You carry with you the message of reconciliation, as if God were making his appeal through you. And you never represent yourself; you always represent God. Why? Because just like Paul, you can say, "I have been crucified with Christ; my old life is gone. Nevertheless, I live. But it's no longer I who live, you see; it's Christ living through me."

"But I'm just a stay-at-home mom." You are not just a stay-at-home mom! You are an ambassador raising the next generation of world changers. You are called by God in your home with a divine mission.

"Yeah, but I'm just a student." You're not just a student! You are an ambassador to your chemistry class; you're an ambassador to your sorority; you're an ambassador to the teachers at your school.

"Well, I'm just an entry-level bank teller." You're not just an entry-level bank teller; you're a secret agent of the most high God, planted in that bank to represent Christ to people that you see all of the time!

When you know who you are, you will know what to do; and you are, if you're a Christian, an ambassador of the Lord Jesus Christ, not elected by people, but called and appointed by God. You never represent yourself, but you always represent him. This is not your home; you're from another country. You represent the king from the kingdom that sent you, the King of Kings and the Lord of Lords, and that makes your role on earth very important. There's nothing regular about you, you see. You are the highest-ranking diplomat sent by God, from the kingdom of heaven, to this earth.

You know who you are.

So you know what to do.

PART 2

Sacrificing Cultural Relativity
for Eternal Values

living
with patience

Patience is the companion of wisdom.

— Saint Augustine

My kids are no different from most kids in our country. To put it bluntly, they're spoiled to one degree or another and are used to getting what they want. So to counteract our culture's insistence on immediate gratification, Amy and I work hard to teach them about the value of sacrifice and delayed gratification. We like to define sacrifice as giving up something that you love for something that you love even more. Instead of getting something that you want today, think how much better it would be to get something that you really, *really* want tomorrow. Why not trade the immediate for the ultimate?

To teach them this principle, I've developed what I call the Oreo Game. Whenever one of my children turns five (old enough to reason well and understand this lesson), I sit them down at the table and place one Double-Stuf Oreo cookie in front of them. Without exception, each chocolate-loving kid dives for the prize. But before the icing-filled cookie hits their drooling mouth, I reach out and grab their hand to stop them.

At first they're always disappointed, until I explain that we're playing a game and I have an offer to make them. I give them their options. "You can eat that one cookie now. It's all yours and you don't have to do anything for it. But that's all you get, one cookie." Then I slide two additional cookies on the table. "But if you wait one hour, instead of just that one cookie, you can have all three." Then I whistle a little game show tune while they try to decide their final answer.

I have one daughter (I won't tell you which one) who always reached for the one cookie. Why wait, right? It took playing the game several times to teach her the value of delayed gratification. Now she's passionate about the benefits of waiting. My oldest son, Sam, on the other hand, was a natural. "That's awesome, Dad!" he shouted enthusiastically. "Let's go play soccer for an hour and then come back and eat the three cookies."

My youngest son, though, might have the most business potential. Instead of taking my initial offer, Stephen negotiated. "How about this, Dad?" he said with his best poker face. "If I wait an hour, why don't you give me *five* cookies instead of three?" Smart kid.

HAVE IT YOUR WAY

Unfortunately, no matter how talented at negotiating we may be, most of us have not learned to wait on our cookies. And it's only after the fact, when we realize what we could've had, that we understand the cost of our decision. We understand that we settled for far less than what God wanted us to have.

It's so easy to live reacting to our impulses, making decisions as if this moment is the only thing that matters. Sadly, so many people remain dangerously shortsighted when it comes to judging what's important and when it is important. While it's good to "be in the moment," many people find it hard to see even two minutes into the future, recognizing the problems their decisions might create.

> It's so easy to live reacting to our impulses, making decisions as if this moment is the only thing that matters.

You've heard the mantras: "If it feels good, do it." "It's my life; I can do whatever I want." "Why should I wait when I can have it now?" Blindly following our entitled egos, we often think we actually deserve whatever we want and should never be forced to wait, plan, prepare, or put something off.

Again, this isn't totally the fault of those who live with this mindset. Strategic marketing, improved technology, and selfish living have trained us well. You grew up on commercials and advertisements that said, "You deserve the best. Have it your way. Live in luxury." Some people believe the microwave triggered a universal lust for now. Zap my problem and it will be fixed in sixty seconds or less. If their iPhone takes more than five seconds to download a site, they get impatient and complain about how pathetic their phone is, or they just go to another site instead.

If you look around, you see it everywhere. A grown man throwing a tirade because his fast food burger took three minutes to make. A mom coming unglued because the high school guy at the cash register slows her down. A young couple becoming furious because they were denied the loan to buy their dream home (which was way over their budget) and they have to do something they've never done before — wait. Our society has trained us that if it is worth having, it is worth having now. If you are going to do it, you should never be forced to wait. In order to feel important, our entitled egos tell us we should get what we want when we want it.

FORBIDDEN FRUIT

While I believe this problem has become progressively worse, it's certainly not new. The Bible is loaded with stories of people who failed to realize the consequences of their short-term decisions. In the very first story in God's Word, Eve craves the forbidden fruit. When you think about it, she has it all — everything any woman could ever desire. An intimate relationship with the God of the universe. A husband who adored her. Paradise as her home.

She also doesn't have some of the things that make us crazy. Eve doesn't have another woman in the world to compare herself with. She never has to wonder, "Do you think she's prettier than me?" She never fears that someone else is a better mom, a better cook, or a better employee, or that someone else has a better body. Eve can't compare kitchens, closets, or husbands; she never has to sink into the trap of comparison envy. The first woman who has ever lived has everything — really everything — except the fruit of the one tree that God said is off limits.

Even though this woman has it all, the serpent still manages to tempt her by asking, "Did God really say, 'You must not eat from any tree in the garden'?" (Gen. 3:1). In our world, the questions might be, "Did God really say you need to wait until marriage until you get to have sex?" "Did God really say that you should love your enemies when you'd rather kill them?" "Did God really say that you should stay married when you'd prefer to be married to someone else?"

Even though Eve has everything but a piece of fruit, the one thing she is denied becomes the all-consuming, gotta-have-it thing.

All of us have reached out to grab some forbidden fruit (or at least a slice of apple pie) and taken a bite that costs more than we ever imagined. Moses did it when he was angry and killed a man. David did it when he was lonely and committed adultery. Judas did it when he became greedy and betrayed Jesus. And we do it when we lose our temper, have sex before marriage, buy something we can't afford, or stuff our faces until we're fat.

We see this common problem described clearly in Scripture: "For the world offers only a craving for physical pleasure, a craving for everything we see, and pride in our achievements and possessions. These are not from the Father, but are from this world. And this world is fading away, along with everything that people crave. But anyone who does what pleases God will live forever" (1 John 2:16 – 17 NLT). People commonly trade the long-term greater blessings that come later for the quick-fix lower things they can have now.

ALL NOW, NONE LATER

If you know anyone who grew up during the Great Depression, perhaps a parent or a grandparent, then you know that their worldview differs radically from that of the generations following them. Because they grew up lacking what we take for granted, they conserved, they saved, and they planned. But those generations coming after the most resourceful generation in recent history have allowed the pendulum to swing to the other side.

Most of my parents' peers (the boomers) borrowed, charged, and leveraged their way to a "better" lifestyle. Now approaching their seventies, that generation is waking up, and their material dream is turning into a financial nightmare. After decades of living for the moment, most are not financially prepared for the later years in their lives.

Unfortunately, the challenges go way beyond finances. During their childhood, divorce was rare. But as they aged, their more self-centered lifestyle led to more self-centered decisions, leaving in their wake damaged or destroyed relationships. My generation, for the most part, followed suit. And those following me have perfected shortsighted living to an art form. My grandma always said, "If you play now, you'll pay later." Unfortunately, there is so much playing now that the payment grows greater even as it approaches us like a bullet.

> With God's help, you can break this curse.

With God's help, you can break this curse.

Let's start by truthfully acknowledging the problem. Wouldn't you agree that it's normal for people to want what they want now, not later? "I gotta have it — now!" "Why wait?" "Nothing is going to stop me from getting what I want!"

This is the exact same attitude of the younger brother in Jesus' story of the prodigal son. Jesus explained that a father had two sons. But the younger of the two didn't want to wait until the appointed time to receive his inheritance, so, the Bible says, "The younger son told his father, 'I want my share of your estate *now* before you die'" (Luke 15:12 NLT, emphasis mine). Like many today, he didn't want to wait. He wanted what he wanted and he wanted it now.

You'll see the same thing all around you, and perhaps even recognize it in yourself. The new associate who's asked to break some ethical standards in order to close the big deal. She feels she has no choice but to go along if she wants to get that promotion and the corner office.

Or maybe it's the guy who's making out with his girlfriend and keeps pushing her, saying, "I've got to have you now or I'll die." Or the woman who sees the perfect pair of shoes that will match the outfit that she doesn't yet have but will buy to match the shoes that she can't afford but must get because they're her favorite designer and are marked down 10 percent. Or maybe it's something more subtle and mundane, like the lonely person who's so disappointed that the presidential debate overrode their favorite sitcom that they ate a whole carton of Cherry Garcia ice cream.

Wanting something that will make you feel better now is something we usually feel we can justify. What's the big deal about a little physical pleasure or a new pair of shoes or a few bowls of ice cream?

The Bible says there is a way that seems right to a man but in the end it leads to death (Prov. 14:12).

DEAL OR NO MEAL

In pursuit of immediate pleasure, people trade the ultimate for the expendable. I heard pastor and author Andy Stanley describe this phenomenon in the biblical story of Jacob and Esau. If you aren't familiar with the story, Jacob and Esau were twin brothers. Esau was the oldest, born minutes before his younger brother, Jacob. I've been told that younger brothers are often jealous of their older siblings, which was certainly the case in this story. Esau was a man's man, while younger Jacob was more of a mama's boy.

During this time in history, the firstborn son had extreme advantages. He had what's known as the birthright. Upon the father's death, the firstborn received twice the inheritance of any of his siblings. He also became the judge (or executor) of the father's estate. Throughout his life, the oldest brother lived with advantages and favor simply because he was born first. You can imagine how this could get under the skin of the younger brother.

Well, with these two guys, the scene went down something like a bad episode of *Iron Chef*. "Once when Jacob was cooking some stew, Esau came in from the open country, famished. He said to Jacob, 'Quick, let me have some of that red stew! I'm famished!' ... Jacob replied, 'First sell me your birthright.' 'Look, I am about to die,' Esau said. 'What good is the birthright to me?'" (Gen. 25:29 – 32).

The conflict seems very basic, a temporary physical appetite battling an eternal familial blessing. Esau, the older brother, has been out hunting and works up a huge appetite. Perhaps his journey home took longer than he expected and his stomach is long past growling. He's not just hungry. He's HUNGRY. When he sees Jacob cooking some stew, Esau demands some lunch.

Suddenly, the younger brother has the advantage, perhaps for the first time ever. I can imagine Jacob, sensing he has the upper hand, thinking, "I've got you now. All those years that you picked on me, all those times you didn't let me play with your friends, all those times you outshined me … now you're going to get yours."

Esau said something that's funny to me. He whined, "Look, I'm going to die if I don't get something to eat." Just in case you're tempted to believe him, let's tell it like it is. He was being a big baby, a drama king, an entitled brat. Esau wasn't about to die. He was just hungry and was used to having food the moment he wanted something to eat.

Jacob corners his brother and strikes a deal. "You want some of this delicious, hot beef stew, with your favorite carrots and tomatoes? Then it's going to cost you. If you give me your birthright, I'll give you some stew."

And that's when Esau makes the worst trade of his life. Esau trades the ultimate (his birthright) for the immediate (a bowl of stew). In the end, he will not be able to put a price on what he pays for a simple meal.

You might ask, "Who in the world would do something as stupid as trade their birthright for a bowl of stew?"

If you think about it, you already know the answer.

We do it every single day.

YOUR BOWL OF STEW

It seems absurd to imagine someone trading something so valuable for something so temporary. Why would Esau make such a bad trade? Why does generation after generation of intelligent adults make similar decisions every day? It's simple. We allow our out-of-control, fleshly desires to overwhelm our better senses. We allow our egos, instead of our altar egos, to drive our desires.

Remember the verse we looked at from 1 John? The world offers to fulfill all our cravings. "I'm hungry and I want it. I'm lonely, so I need that person. I'm empty, so maybe that thing will satisfy me." The world offers substitutes for (or counterfeits of) real things: physical pleasure, material things, pride in what we have and what we do. Before long, our sinful desires for the counterfeits of this world lure us into short-term decisions with long-term consequences.

You unquestionably know lots of people whose lives have been ruined by unchecked and untamed desires. It could be the person who buys things she can't afford, charging and borrowing her way into final fiscal destruction. Each purchase makes her feel good about herself for a fleeting moment; she can wear the latest styles and have the newest phone and iGadget. But one day she wakes up, buried alive under a mountain of debt.

It could be the guy who knows looking at pornography isn't good for his spiritual life or relationships. But when he's tempted with the opportunity, his immediate desire overwhelms his desire to obey God. Before long, what seemed harmless enough at first becomes deadly. He's trapped and believes he can't stop. He had no idea that taking one drink of porn poison would lead to an addiction that slowly kills his soul.

You probably know a young woman who wanted to honor God and her future husband by saving herself for marriage. But since she thought she loved the guy she was dating, and because she didn't want to lose him, she compromised her values by giving her body to him. After her "true love" got what he wanted, he eventually dumped her and moved on to other conquests. At first she felt horrible, but eventually she decided, "Since I'm not a virgin anymore, why shouldn't I find some comfort wherever I can?" And over the years, she accumulated sinful sexual memories, ones that still cloud her marriage and haunt her with regret.

You might know the guy who told himself he'd provide a "better life" for his family. (Have you ever noticed how "better life" never means more time, deeper relationships, or spiritual intimacy? A better life generally means giving them things that won't last and don't really matter.) Armed with good intentions, he threw himself into his career and did whatever it took — sixty-hour weeks, traveling half the month, working at home on weekends. Then one day his company downsized and he found himself looking for a new job. Worse still, he woke up with a failed marriage and children he still sees but doesn't really know.

What have these people and millions of others just like you and me done to ourselves? We've traded the ultimate (God's blessings) for the immediate (our selfish desires). We've given away our birthright for a stupid bowl of stew.

GET THE SCOOP

If trading your birthright for a bowl of stew seems farfetched, then let me share another example. In 1894, the US mint in San Francisco produced only twenty-four coins, relatively few for its time but certainly staggering when we consider the millions of coins produced by our country's mints now. The superintendent of the San Francisco mint then was a man named John Dagget. Knowing the rarity of the few coins produced that year, Dagget acquired several and gave three of the dimes to his daughter, Hallie. "Hold on to these, my dear, and they'll be worth much more than ten cents someday," he told her.

On her way home from her father's office, young Hallie did what many kids would do. She stopped in her favorite soda shop and exchanged what would become one of the world's rarest coins for a scoop of her favorite ice cream. Almost a century later, in 1981, the coin surfaced and sold for $34,100. Today only ten 1894-S Barber dimes are known to exist, and they're considered one of the most sought after coins in the world. Poor Hallie's scoop of vanilla ended up costing her much more than she could ever imagine.

We would be wise to embrace the principle of delayed gratification when it comes to all our finances, not just our dimes. Because of a spirit of entitlement, it's common for teenagers (and adults still in adolescence) to believe they really need the latest iPhone, iPod, or iPad. (If their iPad doesn't have 4G, they need counseling to overcome their childhood abuse.) Some teens actually believe that they need (or deserve) a thirty-thousand-dollar car. Or a debt-ridden twenty-year-old believes a spring break trip to Cancun is a necessity. Or the young couple just out of college feels it is their right to live in a house as nice as their parents' home.

God blessed me with a great professor in college who helped teach me wisdom about money. Dr. Altshuler didn't teach college because he needed the income. He was a very successful, independently wealthy businessman who taught business classes out of his love for the subject and the students.

I asked him for his most valuable piece of financial advice, and his response changed the direction of my life. Without hesitating, Dr. Altshuler said, "Almost everyone your age is going to spend the next ten years buying and accumulating liabilities. If you're smart, you won't do what everyone else does. Wise people don't purchase liabilities; they purchase assets."

Since I was only nineteen and still green around the gills, I asked him to clarify. "What exactly is a liability? And what's an asset?" My professor explained that liabilities are things that depreciate, or go down in value over time. If you buy a car for twenty-eight thousand, it loses at least two thousand in value the moment you drive it off the lot. It's no longer new. Now it's used and worth much less. Within five years, it's worth less than half of what you paid for it.

> **Wise people don't purchase liabilities; they purchase assets.**

Clothes depreciate even more dramatically. A new shirt that costs fifty dollars is worth fifty *cents* at a garage sale a few months later. Same with almost everything that normal people buy. Cell phones go down in value. Computers go down in value. Shoes go down in value. Furniture goes down in value. And trips or experiences that cost hundreds or thousands of dollars don't have any financial value once they pass. That's why most young people end up financially strapped and hurting. They pour all their resources into things that aren't worth much over time.

My wise teacher continued by explaining that life could be totally different if we'd take a long-term approach to managing money. Instead of buying liabilities, we should invest in assets. What's an asset? Something that holds its value, goes up in value, or produces additional revenue. A good stock is an asset. Owning a profitable business is an asset. A house is usually an asset. (I know the housing market has been pounded in recent years, but over time, real estate is generally considered a great investment.)

At the age of nineteen, owning assets seemed unattainable to me. So I asked my professor what type of asset I could ever afford. He explained that he owned rental property, and that perhaps I could buy a small house to live in and have a roommate or two whose rent would cover my payment and perhaps even provide a little more.

I left that conversation and found a house to buy. It wasn't a nice house, by any means, but I was a college guy and used to rough living. Believe it or not, I paid $14,900 for my first house. With a small down payment, my monthly mortgage on a ten-year note came to a whopping $151.77 a month.

I moved in and took in a couple of roommates and immediately was making money. Before long, I bought a second house. I told my buddies that anyone could live in my house for a hundred dollars per guy per month. My friends were so cheap that they'd cram six or seven guys into a two-bedroom house. And in no time at all, I was a nineteen-year-old slumlord making money off my assets.

Over time, I made an enormous amount of money (for a young guy) off my professor's wise advice. While my friends dropped cash on clothes, beer, and cars, I bought cheap houses that paid nice financial dividends. Today, we're able to do way more financially because we bought things that built wealth instead of decreased in value. Later is often better than now.

The same principle is true with sex. Our culture says, "Get it while you can. Why wait until you're married? You wouldn't buy the car without test-driving it first, would you?" So many people trade the ultimate for the immediate. I know I would have, but thankfully Christ transformed my heart and my life before I met Amy. Since we both desired to please God in every way, we were blessed to wait until marriage to share the gift of lovemaking.

Rather than the immediate physical pleasure of premarital sex, we waited and gained the ultimate. This includes a lifelong testimony. I can tell you, our church, our children, and our grandchildren that we honored God by waiting. We also built trust. Had we compromised and had sex before marriage, I would have married a compromiser, and so would Amy. In the back of our minds we might have wondered, "If my spouse compromised before marriage, will he or she compromise again after marriage?"

Instead of fear, we built trust. And our honeymoon? Let's just say God is good. Had we had sex before marriage, our honeymoon would have been just another day at the office. Instead we unwrapped the ultimate gift of intimacy and celebrated marriage as God intended.

THE POWER OF PATIENCE

So how do we move from living like the crowd? How do we overcome the cultural pull toward immediate ego gratification? We pursue God with all of our hearts until his desires become our desires. Rather than craving what our peers crave, we learn the heart of God and long for what matters to him. Our demanding egos become altar egos, with our selfish impatience sacrificed for something far greater.

Scripture instructs us to "take delight in the Lord, and he will give you the desires of your heart" (Ps. 37:4). As we seek God, his desires become ours. The Hebrew word translated as "delight" is the word *anag*. It carries with it the idea of being made soft or pliable. You could say that as we enjoy or delight in God, he shapes our hearts and desires to look like his. Then instead of desiring the cravings of our fleshly nature, we learn to crave the kingdom desires of our God.

All of us want to make a difference in this world. And when we don't have the immediate impact we desire, we often feel frustrated or discouraged as if we've failed at being a Christian. But the truth is that God works in us even when we can't see it — perhaps especially when we can't see it.

One of my mentors told me, "Craig, you'll very likely overestimate what God wants to do through you in the short run. But you will very likely underestimate what God wants to do through you in the long run." He nailed it. I was so disappointed because I didn't see the immediate ministry results that I wanted. I deserved a bigger ministry, didn't I? Truthfully, I didn't deserve anything. I overestimated what I could do in the moment. But I had no idea what God wanted to do through me over a lifetime. Don't give up. Ministry is a marathon, not a sprint.

Paul told us to "let the Holy Spirit guide your lives. Then you won't be doing what your sinful nature craves. The sinful nature wants to do evil, which is just the opposite of what the Spirit wants. And the Spirit gives us desires that are the opposite of what the sinful nature desires" (Gal. 5:16 – 17 NLT). As God's Spirit guides us, we won't be seeking the bowl of stew, another Oreo, or a scoop of ice cream. The Holy Spirit replaces our lower, self-serving, demanding desires with God's higher, kingdom-serving, selfless ones.

Think about this for a moment. For centuries God's name has often been tagged by the patriarchs who loved and served him faithfully. You've probably heard God referred to as "the God of Abraham, Isaac, and Jacob." If you pause and reflect on the story we looked at earlier, you'll see something that will stop you in your tracks.

Esau was the older brother with the birthright. When Jacob tricked him into giving away his birthright, Esau traded the ultimate for the immediate. If he hadn't made that devastatingly destructive shortsighted decision, throughout history you would have heard God referred to as the God of Abraham, Isaac, and *Esau*. Esau lost his standing.

You'll be wiser. I know you will. When faced with temptations, you'll look beyond the moment. You'll remember that patience is better than power. Self-control is more important than conquering a city. You'll choose God's ultimate over the immediate. You'll never trade your birthright for a simple bowl of stew. You'll no longer sacrifice your destiny for distorted desires.

As you realize how much God has planned for you to do in this world, I pray you will live with a long-term perspective, making decisions that will honor God and propel you forward over time. You sacrifice your own ego-driven agenda in order to experience the perfect timing of God's clock. Instead of demanding what you want now, you're often infinitely better off waiting. Proverbs 16:32 says, "Better to be patient than powerful; better to have self-control than to conquer a city" (NLT).

Living with patience is better than muscling forward to demand what you want before the time is right. Self-control often unlocks the door to blessings that are longer lasting and more meaningful. Patience comes from knowing you already have enough of what you need the most.

living
with integrity

*Integrity doesn't come in degrees: low, medium, or high.
You either have integrity or you don't.*

— Tony Dungy

Not too long ago, I went to a convenience store to grab some things, and I handed the cashier a few dollars to pay for my items. She handed me my change and a receipt, and since I was in a hurry, I quickly stuffed them in my pocket and headed out the door. When I was getting situated in my car, I unfolded the money she'd handed me and was about to put it in my wallet when I noticed that she had given me too much change — like, *way* too much.

I'm not going to lie to you. My first thought was, "Wow! God is good!"

Fortunately, my very next thought was, "No! I have to take it back." I'm not sure if it was the voice of my parents from childhood or the whisper of the Holy Spirit nudging my conscience, but I was grateful.

I counted out what the correct change should've been, then went back in the store. Waiting until my generous cashier was free, I stepped up, held out the extra money to her, and said, "Ma'am, excuse me, but you gave me more change than I was due."

She'd been all business, just going through the motions of her job, when suddenly, her entire countenance changed. Her eyes welled up with tears, and she stammered, "Oh, oh, oh my gosh! I cannot *believe* you brought that money back! I just can't believe it!"

She took a second to compose herself. "Thank you so much! This means so much to me. Thank you for doing the right thing! I just can't..."

I was genuinely surprised by what appeared to be her overreaction. I just said, "Really, it's not that big of a deal — "

She interrupted me, "No. No. You just have no idea." She started to come out from behind the counter and she said, "Would you mind if I give you a hug?"

Now I was even more surprised. I said, "Uh ... okay ..." since she was already putting her arms around me. So I did the "pat shoulder, pat shoulder, fade away, break, and we're done" move.

She started back behind the counter, looking at the money in her hand, still overcome with emotion, saying over and over, "I just can't believe you brought it back!"

Welling up with gratitude again, she explained, "This isn't the first time I've done this. I just keep making the same mistake, giving out too much change. Every time it's happened, I've had to pay back whatever I went over. I don't know why it's so hard for me, but it's kept happening." She took a deep breath and lowered her voice. "Since it didn't stop, my boss said, if it happened just one more time, they were going to have to let me go. I'm a single mom. I can't afford to lose this job."

I smiled, turned for the door, and said, "Well, I'm just glad I was able to help you."

Before the door closed behind me, I heard her call out one last time, "I still can't believe you brought that money back! Thank you!"

I don't know who ended up having a better day after that, her or me.

INTEGRITY DEFICIT

Isn't it tragic that we live in a world where people are more shocked by a display of integrity than the lack of it? More and more often, people seem surprised when someone does the right thing instead of when someone fails the morality test. This inversion is a sad indictment of how corrupt and self-absorbed our culture has become. Our ethics become subject to our egos and not the other way around.

You don't have to look far to find story after story about people who lack integrity. Maybe it's a professional athlete everyone looks up to. He's the best at what he does, but on top of that, he selflessly gives of himself to some charitable organization that's making people's lives better. Then one day the news comes out: he had a whole other sordid secret life that we never knew about.

Some politicians do this same thing. They run for office on a platform to make things better, and one day we discover they've been living covertly as though they're above the law. It even happens to Christian leaders — pastors, ministers, evangelists — who preach God's Word but are taking drugs, visiting prostitutes, or embezzling from their churches. It's as if they've allowed their egos to take precedence over their souls.

All of these things are so "normal" that they don't really take us by surprise anymore. It's only worse, it seems, when the same thing happens to a close friend. You thought you knew them. You loved them, trusted them, and then *boom*, the curtain falls and you see the mess that was going on all along behind the scenes.

> Practicing integrity means that your behavior matches your beliefs.

So if the lack of integrity is clear, what is true integrity? Here's a simple definition: Practicing integrity means that your behavior matches your beliefs.

That's all there is to it. All the parts of your life seamlessly form a united whole. There are no secret compartments or double lives. What you say actually matches what you do. Your lifestyle is integrated. Your private life matches your public life, with no surprises. What other people see is what they get no matter the setting in which they meet you. You may have heard the term defined this way: "Integrity is what you do when no one else is looking."

Just to clarify, personal integrity is not the same thing as your reputation. No, your reputation is who other people *think* you are. Your integrity (or lack thereof) is who you *really* are.

God's Word tells us, "The integrity of the upright guides them, but the unfaithful are destroyed by their duplicity" (Prov. 11:3). How true. Just think of all the people who were destroyed when their house of cards — built on the shaky foundation of deception — came crashing down. I think many segments of society are being destroyed today by the duplicity of leaders, even entire organizations, who claim to believe one thing, yet practice something else.

THE WHOLE THING

My wife and I value integrity so much that we remain very intentional about helping our children (and each other) understand and practice it. Our commitment to integrity is even reflected in our children's names. That's why we named our first son Samuel. While it's no coincidence that Amy's dad's name is also Sam, she and I both love the consistency of character we see in the biblical Samuel, from the Old Testament.

Toward the end of his life, Samuel recaps his record of faithful service before the Israelite people:

> "Here I stand. Testify against me in the presence of the LORD and his anointed. Whose ox have I taken? Whose donkey have I taken? Whom have I cheated? Whom have I oppressed? From whose hand have I accepted a bribe to make me shut my eyes? If I have done any of these things, I will make it right."
>
> "You have not cheated or oppressed us," they replied. "You have not taken anything from anyone's hand."
>
> —1 Samuel 12:3 – 4

At the end of his life, Samuel stood before his entire community and said, "Have I lived a life of integrity? If I've ever wronged any of you, just tell me, and I'll make it right."

And they answered him, "No, you've always done the right thing. You are a person of integrity, Samuel. You've been faithful."

At the end of my life, I want to be able to ask the same question and get the same response. I want my children, my grandchildren, generations of Groeschels after me, to be able to do exactly as Samuel's community did. At the end of my life, I want to be able to say honestly, "Here's your free shot. Did I do what I claimed I would do? Did I practice what I preached?"

People may even answer, "Well, we didn't like your cat jokes or the way you dressed or your style of ministry. But, yes, you are a person of integrity. All those things you said you believed you actually lived."

Another biblical man of integrity was David, perhaps made more credible because he failed big time and tried to hide it but in the end couldn't live with himself. He offers another picture of what integrity looks like. In one of his psalms, David asks, "Lord, who may dwell in your sacred tent? Who may live on your holy mountain?" and then catalogs the traits of such a godly person:

> The one whose walk is blameless, who does what is righteous
>   [acts with integrity],
> who speaks the truth from their heart [speaks with integrity];
> whose tongue utters no slander [motivated by integrity],
> who does no wrong to a neighbor, and casts no slur on others
>   [interacts with integrity];

who despises a vile person but honors those who fear the Lord
    [discerns with integrity];
who keeps an oath even when it hurts, and does not change
    their mind [maintains integrity];
who lends money to the poor without interest; who does not
    accept a bribe against the innocent [practices integrity].
Whoever does these things will never be shaken.

— Psalm 15:1 – 5

David asks, "Lord, who gets to enjoy your continual presence? Who gets to walk with you and fellowship with you?" In each case, the answer is the person who lives a life of integrity, and the promise is that "whoever does these things will never be shaken."

When we live this way, we will never be shaken! Do you realize what an incredible statement that is? Based on this passage of Scripture, I'd like to show you four of the direct benefits of living a life of integrity. While there are many more, these are some of my favorites:

1. *You'll walk closely with God.* Think of it like this: If I can
   clearly impart my family values to our children, and they
   choose to live their lives according to those principles, then
   obviously, this will increase our harmony with each other.
   On the other hand, consider what would happen if I clearly
   shared our important values with our children, and one of
   them decided to go his own way, contrary to what we had
   taught him. Now, of course I'll still love that child, but certainly their choices are going to interfere with our intimacy,

our communion, and our ongoing fellowship. Our relationship with God follows a similar dynamic. When you live according to his values, you'll naturally walk with him, enjoying his presence daily.

2. *You'll have divine GPS.* Proverbs 11:3 says that "the integrity of the upright guides them." When you allow integrity to lead you, you don't have to guess about what's right. Decisions become much easier when they're based not on what you think you can get away with but on what's right in God's eyes. It's the difference between following your best guesses on how to reach a destination versus using a first-rate GPS that tells you how to proceed every step along the way. We must allow our integrity to guide us.

3. *You'll feel constant peace.* Probably because of my past, this particular benefit means a lot to me. When I lay my head on my pillow at night, I don't ever lie there worrying, "Man, I sure hope nobody finds out what I've done today." When you live with integrity, you're not constantly looking over your shoulder, fearful of getting caught, wondering how long it will be until you're found out. When you simply do the right thing, you abide in constant peace. There's no fear, guilt, shame, or regret; just peace.

4. *You'll gain trust, respect, honor, and influence.* If you want to lead and inspire your family, be a person of integrity. If you want great children, be a parent of integrity. If you want influence in the business community, be a person of your word. When you live with integrity, people will

follow you and honor you. They'll listen when you speak. Over time, they'll even begin to seek out your wisdom and advice. Such is the legacy of integrity.

PLAYING THE PART

The benefits of integrity may seem obvious, yet they remain out of reach for many people, including those who should be the best examples — Christians. One of the most common complaints I hear from people outside the church is that Christians are a bunch of hypocrites, clearly a problem since a hypocrite is the opposite of a person of integrity. *Hypokrites*, the Greek word that we translate as "hypocrite," means literally "an actor or stage player." In the tradition of ancient Greek drama, each actor played several different roles. They used a different carved wooden mask for each of the various characters they were playing. Maybe you've seen the smiling comic mask alongside the frowning tragic mask used as symbols for the theater or to represent drama in general. When an actor in ancient Greece needed to switch to a different character, he simply picked up a different mask and held it in front of his face. It was as simple as that.

> We present ourselves in the best possible light, even if it's not honest, accurate, or authentic.

I think many of us do exactly the same thing. For each social circumstance we find ourselves in, we present ourselves in the best possible light, even if it's not honest, accurate, or authentic. We calculate who we think someone wants us to be, and then we select the appropriate mask to play that part for them. But it's only a mask. It's not who you really are; it's just who you're pretending to be.

It may be hard to see it in yourself, but each of us lacks integrity at some point or another. But it seems like we can always justify our pet behaviors, whether it's by calling them "little white lies" or telling ourselves that we're protecting the feelings of others. But consider how God looks at our "little quirks." While Jesus openly welcomed repentant prostitutes, adulterers, and other vile sinners into his kingdom, he was relentless in condemning hypocrites. Here's what he says in Matthew 23:25 – 28:

> Woe to you, teachers of the law and Pharisees, you hypocrites! You clean the outside of the cup and dish, but inside they are full of greed and self-indulgence. Blind Pharisee! First clean the inside of the cup and dish, and then the outside also will be clean.
>
> Woe to you, teachers of the law and Pharisees, you hypocrites! You are like whitewashed tombs, which look beautiful on the outside but on the inside are full of the bones of the dead and everything unclean. In the same way, on the outside you appear to people as righteous but on the inside you are full of hypocrisy and wickedness.

Jesus exposed them for what they were. He essentially said, "You fakers. You play actors. You have zero integrity. You put on your game face, and you look religious. You look nice and righteous on the outside. But inside, your heart is absolutely filthy with sin."

It doesn't make any difference if people appear to be righteous. What matters is to be pure on the inside. Woe to you if you lack integrity, full of hypocrisy. We must start with what's inside us, allowing Christ to transform us, and then our actions will follow suit. Through Christ, we clean the inside of the cup before we move on to the outside. We sacrifice our selfish, deceitful, ego-driven impulses on the altar of truth so that our behavior reflects God's righteousness. Integrity starts from the inside out, not the outside in.

> Integrity starts from the inside out, not the outside in.

NET WORTH

Once integrity is established, the issue becomes a matter of saturation. Are we willing to live with integrity in every area of our lives? Or, to consider the question from a different angle, What is your integrity worth?

Of course, it'd be easy to answer, "Oh man, it's worth everything." But don't just jump to an answer. Maybe you really do actually think that. But also consider this: What does your life say? How would your actions answer this question?

For example, let's say you lie on your resume just so you can get a better job. That means that your integrity is worth whatever that job pays. You just took your integrity and said, "I'm willing to trade that for some benefit I think I'll get." That's the true value of your integrity in that situation.

Maybe lying on a resume is too big of a thing for you. You'd never do something that serious. Maybe embezzlement's more your thing. Oh sure, you wouldn't call it that. Let's say you take a ream of paper home from your work every once in a while to use on your printer at home. That means your integrity is worth whatever that ream of paper costs — six dollars? Seven?

Maybe you falsified an expense report. You made a personal expense look like a business expense. Whatever that line item cost, that's what your integrity is worth to you.

Maybe you're married and finances are a little tight, so when you buy an outfit, you hide it for a while. I once heard one woman say, "Sometimes I'll buy an outfit and hide it for two months. Then when I put it on and my husband says, 'Is that a new outfit?' I can honestly say, 'No, I've had it for months!'" Her integrity is worth the price of that outfit. (Just to clarify: if you're thinking, "What a great idea!" then you're missing my point.)

Maybe you're in business, and you occasionally overbill. You do it just a little, and only because you know the client can afford it. Or you cut a few corners here and there in what you deliver. Your integrity is part of the "cost of doing business" that you're secretly asking that client to pay for choosing to do business with you.

Maybe — just with your friends — you exaggerate your stories sometimes, just to make them funnier, or so you get to be the hero.

Maybe you're a student and you really need to get good grades. You want to get into medical school or law school. Or you just need to keep up your GPA, so you cheat on an exam or on a paper just to get by.

What is your integrity worth? I'm not asking what you *think* about integrity or even how you *feel* about it. What I'm asking is this: what does your *life* say your integrity is worth?

A HOLE IN ONE

I've been fortunate to have several key people teach me the real worth of personal integrity. My freshman year of high school, I had a tennis coach named Ken Ellinger. He was one of the best coaches I ever had, but more important, he was an integrity freak.

Our team traveled to a tournament once in another town. The evening before the tournament, we all went out to play miniature golf together. At most of the places I've played miniature golf, at the end of the last hole, when you putt the ball into the hole, it generally goes down a tube and into a locked box. Besides conveniently gathering all of the balls for the course staff, this arrangement has the added advantage that the patrons can't steal the golf balls at the end. Well, this particular time, my buddies and I decided we wanted to keep our golf balls. So on the last hole, we took turns covering it with our foot while another person putted. Each guy positioned his foot, took his count, picked up "his" golf ball, and put it in his pocket.

Later, when we were back at our hotel, everybody had their stolen golf balls put away with their stuff. Everybody except me. I was lying on my bed, my feet propped up on the wall, bouncing my cool purple golf ball off the wall, when Coach Ellinger happened to walk in.

He looked at me, raised one eyebrow, and said, "Craig, where did you get that golf ball?"

I answered back in a way I thought was playful: "Oh gee, Coach … I don't know!"

He said matter-of-factly, "You're off the team."

I sprang up, startled. "Off the team? What? But … why?"

He looked straight into my eyes and said, "If you'll steal a golf ball, you'll steal other things. You don't have integrity. So you're not playing for me."

The gravity of my situation crashed in on me. I begged, "Please, Coach! No! Please! Please don't kick me off the team!"

The disappointment on his face was clear. He held up a hand to silence me. I was on the verge of tears. Then he sighed and said quietly, "Let's go outside."

We walked just a little way down the sidewalk. He motioned for me to sit down. Then he stood over me, looking down at me. For as long as I live, I will never forget that moment. The words that came out of his mouth echo in my mind even today.

> If you have integrity, that's really all that matters. If you don't have integrity, that's really all that matters.

He said firmly, "Craig, if you have integrity, that's really all that matters. And if you *don't* have integrity, well … that's really all that matters."

He stood silently for what seemed like hours. "Do you really want to play for me?"

It was all I could do to maintain eye contact. I nodded once.

"Then here's what you're going to do. You're going to take that ball back. You're going to look the manager right in the eye. You're going to put it in his hand. You're going to tell him you stole it. And you're going to apologize. Do you think you can do that?"

I nodded again, determined not to let any of the tears building behind my eyes escape.

He continued, "Now, you need to understand. You're not doing this for me. You're doing it for you. Living a life of integrity isn't easy. It takes a powerful person. It requires courage. And I want you to live that life."

I did exactly what Coach Ellinger said. I returned that ball and apologized to a very surprised manager. I think about my coach's simple but profound message nearly every day.

If you have integrity, that's really all that matters.

If you don't have integrity, that's really all that matters.

IT'S A RACKET

Just a few years later, I had the opportunity to play tennis in college for a nationally ranked NAIA team. During the summers, I taught tennis lessons to kids to make a little extra money. All of the kids I was teaching were beginners, and at the end of each class, we'd play. To make it fun, I threw out this challenge: "If any of you can beat me, I'll give you my tennis racket."

Now, my racket was very expensive and really nice, but of course they were all new to tennis, so none of them stood a chance. But again, to keep it fun, I'd let our games get really close before I'd finish them off. We'd play to ten points. I'd keep them even with me all the way up to seven or eight, then I'd finish them off. It added a lot of drama, and everybody always seemed to have a really good time.

One afternoon when we were playing, I let one boy get to 8-8, as usual. I intended to shut him out in the next two points. But the very next shot he hit, it just barely rolled over the top of the net and fell on my side. It was a ridiculously lucky shot, almost unheard of at his level. He was jumping up and down, all excited, yelling, "9-8! 9-8! I'm winning!"

I laughed and told him it was a really good shot. Then I talked some trash. "Of course, now I'm gonna have to put you away. I hope your mama's home. You're gonna be running to her crying when I'm done with you."

On the next point, he did exactly the same thing. Again! The ball hit the net, rolled just over the top, and fell on my side! He threw his arms up and started running around, yelling. "It's 10-8! I won! 10-8! You've got to give me your racket!"

All the other kids were on their feet, cheering for him as he danced around like he'd just won Wimbledon. In the meantime, I was thinking very unholy thoughts. "Argghhh! That lucky brat! My best racket! What am I going to do?"

My mind raced for a solution. "Oh, I'll give you my racket, all right. You can have the ancient, cheap wooden racket gathering dust in my garage. Or maybe I'll give you my backup racket, the one that looks like it survived a tornado."

But another voice was haunting me. "Craig, when you have integrity, that's all that matters."

In my head I was screaming, "Shut up! This is my racket, my livelihood! Besides, I was only joking."

I swallowed hard, walked over to the boy, extended my racket to him, and said as earnestly as I could through clenched teeth, "Here's the racket. I ... hope you enjoy it."

I thought this story was over until several years ago. I had just preached a message at our church, and when the service was over, I was standing near the front, visiting with people. A young man came up to talk to me. He looked vaguely familiar, but I couldn't place him. I shook his hand and thanked him for coming.

He started talking really fast and gushed, "Wow, it was like you were talking directly to me this morning. I just prayed that prayer you led us through. I gave my life to Christ! I can already tell that something feels different inside."

Before I could respond, he smiled and said, "You don't remember me, do you?"

I said, "Well, you look really familiar, but I'm sorry, I don't."

"Years and years ago, you taught me tennis lessons one summer—"

I didn't wait for him to finish. "You have my racket!"

He laughed. "No, no! That wasn't me. I don't have your racket. But I was there when it happened. You know, none of us thought you would really give your best racket to that guy. We couldn't believe it when you did! Anyway, when I came here today and I recognized you, I remembered what you did all those years ago. Then I couldn't help thinking that if you were a person of your word then, you're probably a person of your word now. So I really trusted everything you said about Jesus today. And that's why I chose to give my life to him."

NO SPIN ZONE

So when you realize you're not a person of integrity, what do you do? It happens all the time, all around us. A man will be leading a Bible study in his home, but in his "other" life, he screams at his wife and ignores his kids. A married woman is a prayer warrior who serves at the city mission twice a week, even when she's sexting with a guy from her office. A great business leader, a model citizen, is cheating his customers on every deal he makes. A person tells everyone they meet about how they follow Jesus, conveniently leaving out the part about how they're a habitual liar. How can you break old habits and change direction?

To become a true person of integrity, the first thing you have to do is get to know Jesus. I don't mean just to learn about him from a distance, to read nice stories about him. Certainly that can be part of it, but that's only the beginning. You have to get to know him personally. The simple truth is, you can never live a life of integrity on your own. You are bent toward sin. The only way you can do it is to get to know him personally and then allow the indwelling Christ, through the presence and power of his Holy Spirit, to lead you to do what is right. Get to truly know him, and let him start living through you.

Next, you need to set things right. If there are people you've misrepresented yourself to, you need to go to them, repent, and apologize to them. You need to go to each person and admit, "I'm sorry. For the last (however many) years, I have not been true to you. I've been living a life of hypocrisy. Will you forgive me?" If they do genuinely forgive you, you need to understand: just because they forgive you doesn't mean they'll automatically trust you again. You'll have to rebuild — or perhaps build for the first time — your new life of true integrity.

Finally, the hardest thing you need to do is actually the simplest thing. Follow Jesus' direction from Matthew 5:37, where he said, "All you need to say is simply 'Yes' or 'No'; anything beyond this comes from the evil one." You become a walking "no spin zone."

You become a person of your word as you allow Christ to live through you. Don't just try to line up your behavior with your beliefs. Learn what matters to God. Find out his beliefs. And then make them your own.

When you align yourself this way, you'll start walking closely with God and you'll discover you have a built-in guide. You'll find abiding peace. You'll begin to receive honor, trust, and respect from the people around you, and you'll enjoy influence you've never had before. That's where we have to start.

Get rid of the masks. Be the real you. Allow God's Holy Spirit to transform you. Integrity really does matter.

living
with honor

Mine honor is my life; both grow in one;
Take honor from me, and my life is done.

— William Shakespeare

I travel a lot for ministry, occasionally to other countries. Whenever I have a trip overseas coming up, I always consult my friend who's visited more than one hundred different countries. He's my go-to guy for practical cultural advice and gives me a crash course on local etiquette and traditions that I'll need to be aware of in the places I'm going. I learned very quickly that every culture has its own ideas, both about proper ways to show honor and about things you can do that dishonor people.

For example, when my wife, Amy, and I flew to Korea, my friend offered a few simple suggestions. He said, "When you're meeting someone for the first time, it's proper to bow, but just a little. Don't make a big, deep bow; just tilt yourself so that your head is slightly lower than the other person's head. This conveys respect. And when you shake hands, use your free hand to grab your elbow or your forearm as you shake. This gesture is considered very polite, so it's a pretty easy way to show honor."

It's also honoring in Korea to bring gifts. It doesn't have to be something expensive. (And actually, in most cases, something simple is preferred.) And when you offer your gift, you extend it with both hands, and the person receiving it accepts it with both hands. In Korea, as in most places in the world, you have to be careful not to show the soles of your shoes. For example, you must never lift up your feet to rest them on a desk or table, as we sometimes do in the US. (Where I come from, when you do this, it means that you're relaxed and at ease with the person you're with!) Almost everywhere else on the planet, it would be extremely rude.

One day it occurred to me to ask my friend, "If I was coming from another country, visiting the US for the first time, what would you tell me to do to show honor to people here?" Chuckling, he said, "I wouldn't have to tell you anything. Those kinds of things don't really matter to anyone here."

Of course, that's just one guy's opinion. But you have to admit that for the most part, our culture simply doesn't value expressions of honor the way other cultures do. This seems especially true for the younger generation. I've heard many older people bemoan, "The young people don't honor our country. They disrespect our government. They rarely show respect for their elders." While this may fit the stereotypical view of the older generation, they do have a point.

But I'm convinced we all have room for improvement when it comes to living with honor.

HOMETOWN HERO

Why is honor so important? If we look in Scripture, we discover that our ability to honor other people reflects not only how we see them but how we see ourselves — and God. If we look at Jesus' experience, we realize that often those who should give the most honor give the least. Consider what happened when he came back to his hometown after launching his ministry on the road.

Jesus had just returned to his hometown, Nazareth. (Although Jesus was born in Bethlehem, he grew up in Nazareth.) He'd basically been on what we'd call a regional tour, traveling, teaching God's Word, and performing miracles. Jesus had turned water into wine, raised the dead, opened blind eyes, healed deaf ears, and multiplied loaves and fishes to feed thousands of people. He even healed Peter's mother-in-law. (Many scholars believe this is why Peter later

> Our ability to honor other people reflects not only how we see them but how we see ourselves — and God.

denied Christ. Or maybe I'm remembering that part wrong.) Jesus returned to Nazareth fresh on the heels of all of these miracles, but then he hit a wall. We discover that he *couldn't* do these things for his own townspeople because they lacked faith and refused to give him the honor he was worthy of.

Mark 6:1 – 2 says, "Jesus left that part of the country and returned with his disciples to Nazareth, his hometown. The next Sabbath he began teaching in the synagogue, and many who heard him were amazed. They asked, 'Where did he get all this wisdom and the power to perform such miracles?' " (NLT).

In other words, "Wow! This guy is amazing! His teaching is powerful. His miracles are amazing. How is he able to do all of these things?"

Mark 6:3 continues, "Then they scoffed, 'He's just a carpenter, the son of Mary and the brother of James, Joseph, Judas, and Simon. And his sisters live right here among us.' They were deeply offended and refused to believe in him" (NLT).

So in essence they were saying, "Isn't he just that ordinary guy we grew up with? That same Jesus kid from class who was always so annoying? The teacher's pet. He always got perfect scores on every exam. Hey, isn't this the same carpenter guy who made your mom's kitchen table?"

Jesus explained the situation this way: "A prophet is honored everywhere except in his own hometown and among his relatives and his own family" (Mark 6:4 NLT). The Greek word that's translated "without honor" in this passage is *atimos*, which means "to dishonor; to treat as common or ordinary."

Would you like to know how you can have a common or ordinary relationship? Dishonor the other person. Simply treat them as common or ordinary. Take any dating relationship. When couples first get together, being in love comes so easily. Every day is filled with sunshine. And even when it rains, all you see is rainbows. You know

why? Because whether you realize it or not, you're continually showing honor to each other. He opens doors for her. She tells her friends
about all of his great qualities. He brings her presents and flowers. She
bakes him cookies and loves to hear all about his day, every day —
even the boring details!

You demonstrate honor to each other, over and over. But why
doesn't it last? Because couples get married, and they start taking one
another for granted. Instead of continuing to show honor, you start
treating each other as common. What honor once made great, dishonor now makes ordinary.

It probably goes without saying that the opposite of dishonor is
honor. In the Greek, this is the word *time* (pronounced tee-MAY).
Time literally means "to value, to respect, or to highly esteem." It's
usually associated with a way to assign value. It means treating something (or someone) as precious, weighty, or valuable.

For example, I have this basketball that is in every way just an
ordinary, everyday, run-of-the-mill basketball. And yet, it's so valuable to me that I couldn't put a price on it. NBA star Kevin Durant
wrote my name with a short note, then signed his name on a ball that
he gave to me. This gesture made my otherwise ordinary ball extraordinary (at least to me). Once he put his name on it, from that moment
forward, that, not the materials it was made of, is what defined its
value. I would never treat it as common or ordinary.

My family has two common basketballs we use to shoot hoops
at our house. They're in a bin in our garage. Sometimes they get left
outside. Our dog plays with them. We don't care because they're common. But because the name on this other ball has transformed it into

something amazing, unique, valuable, I keep it in a special case. It's in my office, high up on a shelf, safe from harm, in a place of honor and esteem.

That's what honoring does. It esteems and lifts up. Dishonoring devalues and tears down. To honor a person is to believe the best about them and to let them know it. To dishonor a person is to believe the worst and to let others know it. Honor lifts up. Dishonor tears down.

WITHOUT HONOR

Let me give you another example. Years ago, Amy and I were working with this couple. Their marriage was hanging by a thread. When we'd get together with them, over and over again, the wife just continually dishonored her husband. She said mean things about him. She derided him, outlining in minute detail everything she felt was wrong with him.

During one visit, I was formulating how I could tactfully address it, trying to remember what my *Unabridged Pastor's Handbook* had to say about it (that big book you get when you become a pastor that has all the answers in it). But before I could say anything, Amy went straight for the woman's jugular: "You know what I think is the number one reason your marriage is in such bad shape? It's because you constantly dishonor your husband."

Leave it to Amy to tread gently.

The wife went on the defense. "Well, if my husband was one tenth the man your husband is, maybe I'd start showing him honor!"

Amy shot back, "Or maybe my husband is who he is today *because* I've been showing him honor for all these years! And maybe your husband *isn't* because you haven't!"

Honor lifts up, encourages, and builds.

You might think, "I'm not going to show this person honor because they don't deserve it. They're not honorable." But showing honor doesn't work like that. That's mistaking honor for respect. Respect is earned. Honor is given. This is a crucial distinction. You should honor someone just because of the position where God has placed them in your life. We must show honor freely.

It's been my experience that people tend to live up to — or down to — our expectations of them. When you choose to treat people with honor before they're living honorably, often the very honor that you gift them will lift them, to the point that they actually begin living honorably.

Let's finish our story about Jesus' experience and see what a spirit of dishonor does to the Son of God: "And because of their unbelief, he *couldn't* do any miracles among them except to place his hands on a few sick people and heal them. And he was amazed at their unbelief" (Mark 6:5 – 6, emphasis mine).

> People tend to live up to — or down to — our expectations of them.

It doesn't say he *would not.* It says he *could not.* Now, I'm the first to admit that I don't fully understand this. But according to this verse, where there was a lack of faith, where there was a lack of honor, Jesus could not do the very things that he had already done in other places, places where people believed in him and gave him the honor he was due.

I believe that ours is a culture that, for the most part, lacks honor. And Jesus is amazed at our unbelief.

THE HONOR CODE

The Bible says that there are several different groups we should honor. I'm going to focus only on the three that I believe are most important for you to become all God wants you to be.

First, we're supposed to honor our parents. The Bible is incredibly clear on this one. It's so important, God actually included it in his top ten in Exodus 20:12: "Honor your father and your mother, so that you may live long in the land the LORD your God is giving you."

So often, the opposite happens. I can't tell you how many times I've seen teenagers (and even children) speak disrespectfully to their parents. It seems like some kids even go out of their way to dishonor their parents, trashing them online or even to their faces. And our culture seems to celebrate this behavior, often playing it as comedy.

Maybe I'm just old-fashioned, but at my house, when we ask a child to do something, there's only one acceptable response: "Yes, sir!" if it's to me, and "Yes, ma'am!" if it's to my wife. (Full disclosure: there was a time when my youngest daughter, Joy, was still working out this system, and I was willing to accept "Yes, ma'am!" from her.)

And this verse doesn't apply just to children. God doesn't give an upper age limit on honoring our parents. We don't do it just when we're little kids. We continue doing it when we're in our twenties, our thirties, our forties, our fifties. If you have children yourself, a good way to demonstrate honor to your parents is to speak well of them in front of their grandchildren. Maybe your parents didn't live honorable lives. Maybe your dad ran off with another woman. Maybe your mom struggled with substance abuse. Whatever their circumstances, it really doesn't matter. It's respect that people have to earn; honor is a gift that you give freely. (Besides, if it wasn't for them, you wouldn't even be alive right now.) Find ways you can honor them, not just because they deserve it but because it's the right thing to do.

The next group that the Bible says we ought to show honor to includes those who are in authority over us. Romans 13:1 – 7 explains that God, in his sovereignty, has placed people in positions of leadership. In this context, verse 7 says that you should "give to everyone what you owe them: If you owe taxes, pay taxes; if revenue, then revenue; if respect, then respect; if honor, then honor." (Notice that this verse makes a distinction between respect and honor again.)

Last year, I was invited to speak at a leadership event that was to span several days. I spoke on Thursday. Then on Friday, former president George W. Bush and his wife, Laura, were scheduled to speak. That Friday afternoon, as we were waiting for the president and the first lady to arrive, I was visiting casually with the gentleman seated next to me. I learned that he was not a fan of President Bush — at all. He told me, "I didn't vote for him. I never liked him. I didn't agree with his policies." But that was just the warm-up. This guy went on and on, specifying the things he didn't approve of and why.

Suddenly a door opened and a soldier walked in, carrying the flag of the United States of America. "Hail to the Chief" began to play, and everyone in the room rose to their feet, cheering and clapping. The president walked in, holding the first lady's hand. I glanced sideways at this man standing next to me, the man who couldn't stand the guy, and tears were streaming down his face. He was clapping and smiling broadly.

In that moment, my neighbor was no longer a Democrat or a Republican. He wasn't a fan of President Clinton or of President Obama, and he wasn't a critic of President Bush. He was simply a citizen of the United States, freely offering honor, if not to the man, then at least to the office. The feeling in the room was electric. Everyone there showed honor.

HONORABLE MENTION

We're supposed to show honor not only to powerful people in government but to all of those who are in authority over us. If you play sports, show honor to your coach. If you're a student, honor your teachers. If you have a mentor, show them honor.

Honor your boss. Even if you believe deep down that you're smarter than your boss, you still need to show that person honor. Maybe you'd like to be the boss someday. Before you can learn to be over, you have to learn to be under. Practice being under by showing honor to those people whom God has put over you.

If you're a married woman, but you don't particularly like your husband — maybe he's not the leader that you want him to be — honor him. If you treat him as ordinary and common, he won't feel empowered to lead your family. But if you honor him, give him the opportunity to rise to the occasion, to become honorable. Treat him like he's the man you want him to be; with grace and honor, help him envision himself as a better man.

The third group God calls us to honor is pastors and church leaders. The Bible tells us that we are to show honor to those who are spiritually instructing and discipling us: "The elders who direct the affairs of the church well are worthy of double honor, especially those whose work is preaching and teaching" (1 Tim. 5:17).

This sounds easier to believe than it is to practice. A few years ago, I was consulting with a church that was struggling through some severe issues. For about eight years, they had been in steady decline. During one of our consultations, I met with the senior pastor, together with his elders, so we could try to figure out what was going on. During this meeting, every time the senior pastor spoke, the elders dishonored him. They constantly interrupted him and cut him off. They spoke over him. He tried to float an idea, and one of them scoffed and said something like, "We've already tried that! It doesn't work!" This continued throughout our entire meeting. After everyone had had an opportunity to share their views about what was wrong, they turned to me. "So, Pastor Craig, what do you recommend?"

I imagine they thought I was going to say something like, "You need to start a contemporary service," or, "You need to restructure," or, "You need a better location."

The answer was much simpler.

I said, "I'm pretty sure I know the problem. The reason why God has not been blessing your work here is that you're not showing honor to the person whom God has called to lead you." I reminded them of 1 Timothy 5:17.

At first, they argued. "No, no, that's ridiculous!"

This time it was me who interrupted. "No. Let me repeat to you some of the things you said in the last hour." Then I pointed out specific instances in which they had shown dishonor to their leader. I calmly recounted how he suggested something, and one of them contradicted him. I gave them examples of when they interrupted him or just spoke louder to drown out what he was saying. I explained, "When you discredit your pastor, you're devaluing the office God has placed him in. You're clearly telling him that you don't believe in him. You're stripping away the power that he needs to lead you effectively."

The truth of it hit them all at once. The room was really quiet for several minutes, as they exchanged glances with each other and looked down at the table. One of them lifted his head to meet my gaze and said quietly, "You're absolutely right. I don't know why I couldn't see it before."

And one by one, each man took turns apologizing to their pastor. They repented for not speaking well of him and for not supporting him. They committed themselves to a new course under his leadership, and they agreed to hold each other accountable.

During the next four years, as they showed honor to the position of authority that God had placed over them, spiritual renewal came to that place, and their church doubled in size under a more confident, Spirit-led pastor. Giving honor where it is due has tremendous power.

When you show honor to those who lead you spiritually, I guarantee you that they will take very seriously the role that God has placed them in.

HONOR ROLL

Since most of us have been raised in a dishonoring culture, how can we grow in honor? The English Standard Version of the Bible translates Romans 12:10 like this: "Love one another with brotherly affection. Outdo one another in showing honor."

So it's really that simple. Take that verse to heart, and not only show honor to other people but try to *outdo* one another in showing honor. What does that mean? That means that you go out of your way to demonstrate honor to them. Whether they deserve it or not (and honestly, many won't), you give it out freely. Treat honor like it's the most renewable resource on the planet.

If there are people who take care of your children during the week while you work, show them honor. Find out their names. Learn their birthdays. Bring them gift cards and handwritten thank-you notes. When a person serves you, whether at a business or a restaurant, make a point to be overly courteous to them. Tell them that you appreciate what they do. Offer them some encouragement and a smile. Tip generously. Ask them if there's anything you can pray for them for. If they give you something to pray about, then pray for them.

> Try to *outdo* one another in showing honor.

At your church, single out the people who serve you. Thank them. Show them honor. Write a note to those who minister to your kids. Bring a gift to your small group leader. Email the worship pastor to say thanks for helping you grow closer to God through worship.

Outdo one another in showing honor.

Earlier I told you how you could have a common or an ordinary relationship. Let me tell you how you can build a great one. And this applies to *all* relationships, whether spouse to spouse, child to parent, friend to friend, whatever. Lean in. Listen closely. *Outdo* each other. Lift them up. Encourage them. Esteem them highly. Tell them you value them, and then demonstrate it by your actions. You might just be surprised to see them grow into what you speak to them in faith.

Although I may not know you personally, I honor you for reading this book. Not because you're paying good money to read something I wrote or because you're inflating my ego by telling everyone how good this book is on your Facebook page. No, seriously, I honor you because if you're reading this book and have gotten this far, then you are serious about wanting to be more like Christ. You are serious about wanting to overcome your naturally selfish, ego-driven motives and replace them with godly, altar-ego-driven motives. I commend you.

GOD'S AUTOGRAPH

I'm convinced that the reason our culture is known worldwide as a place of dishonor is that we, as a culture, have dishonored God. All true honor is born out of a heart surrendered to the King of Kings. Psalm 22:23 says, "You who fear the LORD, praise him! All you descendants of Jacob, honor him! Revere him, all you descendants of Israel!"

Our culture tends to treat God as common. We're too familiar with him. We refer to him as "the Man Upstairs" or "the Big Guy," or we say things like "Jesus is my homeboy." Jesus is *not* your homeboy.

He is the soon-to-return, ruling, reigning King of Kings and Lord of Lords. He is the Alpha and the Omega. When he returns, it will be with a sword. He is the Righteous One who shed his blood so that we would live.

We have to stop treating God as common or ordinary. When we're able to see him as he is, we'll honor others not because we want to be good people but because his name is on our hearts. We're no longer common or ordinary, because having his name on us makes us valuable. We have God's autograph written across our hearts just as a great painter would sign his masterpiece.

Or consider the value of his signature another way. Babe Ruth is, to this day, considered one of the greatest — if not *the* greatest — home-run sluggers of all time. During his career, the Great Bambino autographed many baseballs, but he put his name on only seven of the bats he'd used to hit home runs. Because he autographed so few, each of these bats is exceptionally valuable. The first of the bats vanished into thin air, lost for decades. Only when it resurfaced in 2006 was its story discovered.

The bat, used to hit a home run in Yankee Stadium against the Boston Red Sox on April 18, 1923, was given away by Ruth's agent as a prize in a home-run contest. No one at the competition got the address of the winner, so when he left with his bat, it disappeared from the public eye.

In 1988, the man was sick on his deathbed, losing the battle to a prolonged illness. He had outlived every member of his family, and his closest friend was a faithful nurse who'd served him for years during his sickness. Before he died, the man presented his nurse with

his prized autographed bat. Although this gesture carried great senti-
mental value, she had no idea it was actually worth anything. For the
next eighteen years, she kept it under her bed.

After retiring from nursing, she hoped to open a restaurant, but
she didn't have any money. One day she thought of her bat and wondered if it might be worth something. She took it to a sports memo-
rabilia shop to have it appraised. When the owner suspected it might
be the missing Babe Ruth bat, he brought in several experts. After
hearing her story and carefully testing its condition and provenance,
they determined it was the real deal.

In 2006, she auctioned off the bat through Sotheby's for almost
1.3 million dollars.

The woman kept only as much of the money as she needed to
start her restaurant, then gave the rest to begin a foundation to serve
the kinds of children Babe Ruth wanted to help at the end of his life.

When a reporter asked her why she would give away so much of
her money, she answered, "The bat was valuable only because Babe
Ruth's name was on it. Since he made it valuable, the only reasonable
thing I could do was something that would honor his life."

If you're a Christian, what makes you valuable is the name of
Jesus written on your heart. Because of what he did for us on the
cross, our only reasonable response is to do something with our lives
that honors him. Sadly, the Bible describes a truth that is much more
common: "The Lord says: 'These people come near to me with their
mouth and honor me with their lips, but their hearts are far from
me'" (Isa. 29:13).

That won't be us. That won't be you. We will not be a generation that gives God only lip service. Instead, we'll show him honor from our hearts. It's because of what he did that we are who we are. We should value others and show them honor, and we should help them see that they were valuable enough for Jesus to give his life for. Living with honor reminds us of who we really are, who God is, and how much he loves those around us. When we place our selfish egos on the altar of honor, we become aware of the value that God places on each and every life, including our own.

chapter 8

living
with gratitude

*Feeling gratitude and not expressing it
is like wrapping a present and not giving it.*

— William Arthur Ward

It was about three weeks before Christmas, and I was one of the thousands of people braving the crowds searching for the perfect gift for the person who already has everything. As I politely tried to navigate the sea of shoppers in the big-box electronic store, we all stopped in our tracks when we heard a young girl screaming at the top of her lungs.

Is she hurt? Lost? Being kidnapped?

Instinctively, I dropped the video game that I had selected for one of my kids and dashed two aisles over toward the shrieks to see if I could help. Evidently most everyone else in the store had the same idea, because suddenly a crowd formed as we all rushed to the scene.

The little girl, maybe eight or nine years old, wore dark-pink, knee-length shorts with a matching lighter pink T-shirt with "I'm Cute, Spoil Me!" written across the front. Under different circumstances, I'd say the "I'm Cute" part of her shirt would have been true. She was missing a front tooth, and her blond, curly hair was pulled back in a ponytail.

"I want the new one and I want it now!" she shouted and cried all at the same time as she kicked the floor with her pink Crocs, arms flailing wildly.

All of us in the small crowd that had formed were in shock.

The girl continued to flail violently, squirming and seemingly fighting for her life. But she was only fighting for a new gadget, wrestling her mother, a normal-enough looking woman who was clearly mortified. The girl looked like she was auditioning for the role of spoiled heiress in a new Willy Wonka movie, or perhaps to be more accurate, the demon-possessed child in a remake of *The Exorcist*. She was that bad. To say she was throwing a fit is the understatement of the century.

"I will hate you forever if you don't get me the new one!" she screamed, launching a bloodcurdling wail toward her helpless mom.

Security showed up, and the mom, embarrassed beyond measure, broke down and surrendered. "Okay, okay, okay," she said, obviously losing a battle that she'd lost before. "I'll get you the new one if you'll just calm down. Please ... just ... calm ... down."

Instantly, the little girl's mood changed. Like an actress who had just finished her scene, the girl stood up, straightened her clothes, and caught her breath. Then she said very calmly, "Well, then, that's more like it. And I want the red one."

To this day I'm not sure what new thing the girl wanted. Evidently she had at least one of the older versions, but it obviously no longer did the trick for her. Thankfully you won't see a scene like that every day you go out shopping. But you've likely seen something sadly similar. The kid in the line at the grocery store who demands a pack of gum, a Snickers candy bar, or a Buzz Lightyear toy. Or the twins who kick, scream, and throw a fit when they refuse to leave the theme park. Or the teenager who yells at his parents, slams the front door, and speeds away in his car because they won't let him stay out past midnight. Or the adult who demands to see the manager when they can't get into a crowded restaurant.

You can see them at every stage of life, although you do wonder if it starts in childhood. With the purest of motives to give their children a better life, many parents directly or indirectly spoil their kids by giving them everything they demand. The kids grow up to be unhappy adults, still chasing the next trend or looking for a bigger house, a faster car, or a better-looking spouse. They raise their kids with the same never-enough mindset. Growing up with a spirit of entitlement inflates our egos temporarily but at the expense of one of the most important virtues to be successful in life — the gift of gratitude.

ONE IN TEN

I believe the loss of gratitude has gotten worse in recent years. But by no means is it a new problem. Jesus told a story in Scripture that illustrates the tragedy of the ungrateful heart. "Now on his way to Jerusa-

lem, Jesus traveled along the border between Samaria and Galilee. As
he was going into a village, ten men who had leprosy met him. They
stood at a distance and called out in a loud voice, 'Jesus, Master, have
pity on us!'" (Luke 17:11 – 13).

To grasp the full impact of this story, you must understand that
leprosy was one of the cruelest, most repulsive incurable diseases of
Jesus' time. The disease ate away at the flesh of a helpless person.
Daily their sores oozed. When a leper tried to sleep at night, rats or
other rodents attempted to gnaw on the exposed bones of the infected
person. It wasn't uncommon for the poor soul to awaken with a missing finger or toe, lost to some rodent.

Although their pain at times was unbearable, the emotional
wasteland lepers experienced likely was even more excruciating. Not
only because of their gruesome appearance but also because their
condition was contagious, the infected people were banned from society and forced to live outside cities in leprous colonies. Anytime anyone approached a leper, the diseased victim had to shout, "Unclean,
unclean!" warning approaching people of his condition.

You can imagine how difficult it would be to go weeks, months,
years, or even decades without a touch, a hug, or an embrace. It's no
wonder that after hearing about the miracles of Jesus, when the lepers
saw Jesus approaching, they shouted at the top of their lungs, "Help
us! Please help us! Have pity on us!"

In his mercy, Jesus showed the lepers compassion. "When he saw
them, he said, 'Go, show yourselves to the priests.' And as they went,
they were cleansed. One of them, when he saw he was healed, came
back, praising God in a loud voice. He threw himself at Jesus' feet and

thanked him — and he was a Samaritan. Jesus asked, 'Were not all ten cleansed? Where are the other nine? Has no one returned to give praise to God except this foreigner?'" (Luke 17:14 – 18).

Imagine this. Ten lepers suffered desperately. Ten lived in dire need of help. Ten pleaded and begged for mercy. And ten were healed. But only one returned to offer thanks. Their lives, their relationships, their potential, and their destinies were forever altered by the Son of God, but nine couldn't find the time or make the effort to express love, worship, or gratitude. Only one returned to offer thanks. Nine received the answer to their greatest prayers and ignored the one who gave it.

CULTIVATE THE VALUE OF GRATITUDE

Have you ever gone to a lot of trouble to do something special for someone, but they barely acknowledged your effort? You planned. You saved. You prepared. You thought of every detail. You made everything just right. You worked like crazy to surprise someone, bless someone, honor someone. And they didn't say thank you. Of course you didn't do it to be rewarded, but an acknowledgment would have been nice.

Imagine how God feels when he gives us life, his love, his presence, his blessings, his Son. And we ignore him, continuing to do our own thing. Or perhaps we're a bit more gracious and give a polite, token "thanks, God." We show up for church once or twice a month, if we're not too tired or don't have the chance to take a weekend trip out of town. We halfheartedly sing a few songs, listen to the sermon, nodding to acknowledge God before rushing to our favorite restaurant to enjoy our normal life.

I promise you that to honor God and maximize his potential for you, you'll need to learn and live, embrace and cultivate the life-changing value of gratitude. Gratitude kills pride. Gratitude slays self-sufficiency. Gratitude crushes the spirit of entitlement. When we place our discontented egos on the altar of gratitude, we develop contented altar egos filled with thanksgiving.

> When we place our discontented egos on the altar of gratitude, we develop contented altar egos filled with thanksgiving.

Learning to be grateful to God puts us in a constant awareness of the source of all good things in our lives, always reminding us of our need, which God met through Christ. Rather than demanding that God serve our wishes, gratitude puts us in our rightful place — eternally indebted to the one who gave us life.

When you dig up the roots of entitlement, gratitude will grow in the good soil of a fertile heart. Gratitude will change how you see your past, acknowledging God's sovereignty in all things. Gratitude positions you to experience God moment by moment in the present, depending on him daily. Gratitude places you in a posture of worship, ready to give praise to God for every good thing he will do in your future.

What has God done in your life? What has he given you? What blessings do you take for granted? Your life? Your health? Your friendships? Your job? Your home or apartment? When you pause to really think, I promise you can see God in all things, even in the things you wish had never happened.

I've always found it interesting that people ask why bad things happen to them, but they rarely ask why good things happen to them. These attitudes reflect the false belief that we don't deserve bad but we do deserve good. Remember, all we really deserve is hell. If you're a Christian, Christ has saved you from the pit of your sin. You've been filled with the Spirit of God. You're adopted into God's eternal family. Your life is not your own. You were bought with a price — the blood of Jesus shed for you on the cross.

Just like the lepers, you've been cleansed. Healed. Transformed. Will you be like most in our society — like the nine who are too busy to say thank you? Or will you be different, live gratefully, and return to say thank you to the God who gave you everything that matters?

THE UNGRATEFUL DEAD

Remember the little girl who threw the fit to get what she wanted, proving she was ungrateful for what she already had? Most of us, at one time or another, have a similar little voice inside of us. "I want it. Now. I deserve more. I deserve better. Why does she get all the breaks? Why don't I get what I have coming to me? It's not fair." The ungrateful voice inside of us demands more and ignores the blessings God gives. What are we doing? We're resenting God's goodness in someone else's life and ignoring God's goodness in our own.

One time we were raising money for a new playground for the kids at our church. You may have seen these colorful wonderlands in parks where you live. They've got slides, swings, climbing walls, curved balance beams, and monkey bars. (Not only do my kids love these playlands, but I've been known to climb on top and have a bit of fun myself.)

Knowing our church's parents would be excited to get behind this project, I recorded a simple video to show an example of the playground we'd get for our kids. When the video was almost over, I looked into the lens and said, "Let's give big because our kids deserve the best."

At the time, I didn't think anything of the video. It looked good. Sounded good. Felt good. Until my good friend approached me after watching the video during one of the weekend services at church. Steve had just returned from a mission trip to a very poor part of the world. The people in the village he served didn't have running water, plumbing, or electricity. They fought daily to get enough food to survive. Most people died early, either from starvation or some treatable sickness. Steve told me all about the trip and showed me pictures of the kids that had nothing. Then he said, "Next time you make a video to raise money for a luxury like a very expensive playground, maybe you shouldn't say that our kids 'deserve' it. They really don't."

Steve was right. Without even knowing it, I've been sucked into an entitled, demanding, and ungrateful culture. I *deserve* my pizza delivered to my home in thirty minutes or less. I *need* a phone with an unlimited data plan or I can't function. I *have* to have an SUV to keep my family safe. I've *got* to have the $120 pair of jeans. My kids *must* be in soccer, dance, and piano.

Without knowing it, we take for granted all our luxuries and whine like spoiled brats when we don't have the new tech gadget or pair of shoes that we really desire. We never stop to say, "Thank you, God, that I have a toilet — in my house — one that actually flushes." "Thank you for air conditioning in the summer and heat in the winter." "Thank you for my health, my friends, my church." Just like the nine lepers, we take what God gives us and never express true gratitude.

Like the older brother in the story of the prodigal son, if we don't have what someone else does, we think life is not fair. God is not fair. If you know the story about the father and two sons, once the younger son returned home, the father decided to throw a big party. He gave his returned son a ring, killed a cow, and invited everyone in town to celebrate. (In our culture, he would have iced down the soft drinks, hired a DJ, ordered a big cake, and put the burgers on the grill.) But the ungrateful older brother, who already had everything, complained. "Look! All these years I've been slaving for you and never disobeyed your orders. Yet you never gave me even a young goat so I could celebrate with my friends" (Luke 15:29).

Can you hear the same attitude all around you today? "Someone owes me. I deserve better. I should have a company car. A better salary. The nicer office. I should be married by now. Why can't I have a bigger house? With a three-car garage? A walk-in closet? And granite countertops? I shouldn't have to drive this old car. Mine should be brand new. Besides," (you have to walk into a full closet full of clothes and run your hand along them for this one to work), "I've got *nothing* to wear."

> To overcome our dissatisfied, ungrateful attitude, we must first identify it in specific areas of our lives.

And God is certainly grieved by our ingratitude.

ENOUGH IS ENOUGH

To overcome our dissatisfied, ungrateful attitude, we must first iden-tify it in specific areas of our lives. Truth is, ungratefulness is often difficult to see in ourselves, sort of a blind spot to the blessings we have. I'm going to walk you through a few different common catego-ries of ungratefulness to help you expose any ungratefulness hiding in the dark parts of your heart. Let's name the areas of ungratefulness, because you cannot defeat an enemy that you cannot name.

Are you materially or financially ungrateful? Are you disap-pointed that you don't have more things, newer things, or nicer things? Do you occasionally or often complain about your salary, your house, your clothes, or your car? Do you get jealous when someone else gets something that you don't have? Travels to a place you'd like to go? Or wears the outfit you can't afford? Do you have everything that you really need, but wish you had more? If so, you probably battle with financial or material ungratefulness. Admit it. Name it. Call it what it is. There is a part of your heart that needs cleansing.

How about when it comes to relationships? Are you jealous because your best friend has a boyfriend and you don't? Or because most all of your friends are married and you aren't? Or because you see someone else with a good marriage, and both you and your spouse know that yours isn't good at all? Maybe you've been left out of a group you'd love to be in and it hurts you. Maybe someone has gotten closer to the person who used to be your best friend. Sure, you've got some friends, but they aren't enough. You're relationally ungrateful. You don't want to admit it, but it's true. Own it.

Perhaps for you, it's circumstantial ungratefulness. You don't like your hair. Or your body. Or the city you live in. Or the climate. It's too hot or too cold, or too muggy or too dry. For you, it might be the company that you work for. They don't offer great benefits. They take you for granted. You're just a number to them. You're sick of working all the time, especially since you are so underpaid.

You wish your life were different, but you feel trapped. The truth is you have a lot to be thankful for. But you rarely stop to think about those blessings because you have so many other dissatisfactions. Don't shake it off. If it's true, admit it. You're circumstantially ungrateful.

Once you identify the darkness, you can invite the light of Christ to change you. You might think, "This is just the way I am. I'm just not a naturally grateful person. I'm more of a glass-half-empty type of person." That may be true, but God can change you.

TURN BACK TO PRAISE

How do you overcome the seeds of ungratefulness that culture has planted in your soul? How do you learn to be grateful in a world that excels at its opposite?

I'd like to borrow a line from a Matt Redman song called "Blessed Be Your Name." In it, he sings to God, "Every blessing you pour out, I'll turn back to praise." To cultivate an attitude of gratitude, we should turn everything good in our lives into an opportunity to worship. When we do, we're acknowledging the giver of the gifts. The Bible says in James, "Every good and perfect gift is from above" (1:17). Since anything good we have comes from God, why not give God the credit?

Remember the entitled person feels he deserves everything good that he receives, ignoring God's goodness in the blessings. But when he doesn't get what he wants in life, God tends to get the blame. On the other hand, when we turn blessings to praise, we cultivate gratitude. We're training our hearts to become constantly aware of God's goodness.

Any blessing we don't turn back to praise turns into pride. We think we earned it, deserved it, or are worthy of it. That's pride. And pride breaks God's heart. Among other things, pride is a God-repellent. He opposes the proud. The good news is that God gives grace to the humble. Just as pride disgusts God, praise delights him.

The apostle Paul modeled the right attitude better than anyone I know. Paul easily could have fallen victim to material, relational, or circumstantial ungratefulness. He had reason to gripe about all that he'd given up for Christ. He'd surrendered the normal life of marriage and being a dad to spread the gospel. He'd been beaten, flogged, shipwrecked, stoned, left for dead, and imprisoned.

While in house arrest, instead of blaming God, crying about the injustices, or losing his faith, Paul chose to focus on what he had. In his gratitude, Paul discovered the secret of contentment. This wasn't a natural response for him, just as it won't be natural for us. Paul had to learn contentment, gratitude, and praise. He said, "I have *learned* to be content whatever the circumstances. I know what it is to be in need, and I know what it is to have plenty. I have *learned* the secret of being content in any and every situation ... I can do all this through him who gives me strength" (Phil. 4:11 – 13, emphases mine). No matter what life threw his way, Paul learned to be grateful and content. Not on his own but through Christ who gave him strength.

Once you take inventory of all your blessings, it's easy to be thankful for what God has given you. But it's also helpful to think not just of the good things you have but also the bad things that you haven't experienced.

In her poem "Otherwise," poet Jane Kenyon reflects on her blessings with gratitude, embracing each moment of life.

I got out of bed
on two strong legs.
It might have been
otherwise. I ate
cereal, sweet
milk, ripe, flawless
peach. It might
have been otherwise.
I took the dog uphill
to the birch wood.
All morning I did
the work I love.

At noon I lay down
with my mate. It might
have been otherwise.
We ate dinner together
at a table with silver
candlesticks. It might
have been otherwise.
I slept in a bed

in a room with paintings
on the walls, and
planned another day
just like this day.
But one day, I know,
it will be otherwise.

Kenyon wrote this poem in 1993, upon learning that her husband, Donald Hall, had cancer. Ironically, it was Kenyon, not Hall, who died a year later after a fierce and swift battle with leukemia. "Otherwise" came unexpectedly. But Jane Kenyon didn't miss the blessings of God in each day. She learned the art of gratitude.

A DIFFERENT PERSPECTIVE

Like the apostle Paul, I too had to learn gratitude in all things. Truthfully, I'm not naturally grateful. I'm embarrassed to say it, but I'm bent more toward the negative, critical, discontented, and ungrateful side. Because I'm a pastor, people give me way more credit than I deserve. Like the time I spent the night with a friend. When his alarm clock blared at 5:00 a.m. the next morning, I was so annoyed I shouted, "Turn off the alarm!"

Later that day, he told me he was so blessed by what I did when the alarm sounded. "What did I do?" I asked, not remembering anything special. "At the crack of dawn, your first words were, 'Good morning, Lord!'" He didn't have good hearing, and I never told him that I really shouted in annoyance, "Turn off the alarm!"

One verse that helped build in me a spirit of gratitude is Ecclesiastes 6:9, which says, "Better what the eye sees than the roving of the appetite." Think about it. Wanting what you have is better than trying to have what you want. It's better to embrace what God has given us than to whine about what he hasn't. When you take every good thing and acknowledge it, giving praise to God, it radically changes your perspective.

Turn your blessings into praise. Instead of complaining about your older car, you can thank God every day that you have transportation. If your house is always a wreck, you can thank God that you have a family, kids, and toys. If you feel like you're always busy running from one place to another, you can thank God that you're healthy, needed, and have the ability to live an active, productive life. If your house is small, you can thank God that you have a refrigerator, a bed, and running water. If you don't like your job, wake up every day and remember all of the people who would kill for your job. Then thank God he has provided you with employment. Perspective is everything.

> **Wanting what you have is better than trying to have what you want.**

LOST AND FOUND

Some experiences remind us about our perspective in very dramatic ways. One time our family traveled from Oklahoma to Florida for some fun in the sun. Unfortunately, we were there the week the sun went on vacation and the weather was horrible. Rain, rain, and more rain. After several days of indoor activities, I was really upset that we spent so much money and traveled across many states to vacation in weather worse than we had at home. Finally, the weather slightly improved. Not much, but enough to play on the beach — sort of.

Since the storm was lingering, we couldn't let our kids go more than knee deep in the ocean. The waves, riptide, and undertow looked too much for our small, young children, who were rookie swimmers from Oklahoma. With *Baywatch*-like lifeguard skills, still grumbling under my breath about the bad weather, I watched every move the kids made in the ocean. *Stupid weather.*

For a moment my mind wandered, imagining the most beautiful day at the beach — the one I was certain would show up the day we left for home. When I came out of my short daydream, I counted kids. One, two, three, four, five ... *five*? Where's number six? My heart skipped a beat. I quickly did an inventory. There's Catie, Mandy, Anna, Sam, and Joy. Where's Stephen?

Time froze.

I ran full speed into the choppy ocean, screaming for Stephen. Amy and all the other children panicked with me and switched into search-and-rescue mode. We screamed and prayed to God for mercy. With prayers flying nonstop, we continued calling for him, watching for any sign of our smallest son in the water.

Nothing.

Seconds turned into minutes. As each second passed, our fear skyrocketed. Other people came running to join the search. We feared that our lives had just been forever altered for the worse.

That's when Catie, my oldest, pointed over the sand dune and screamed, "Stephen!" with relief in her voice. Little Stephen walked slowly over the dune, pulling up his pants, attempting to tie the drawstring on his swim trunks. Evidently Stephen had to "go," so he found a tree and relieved himself.

Upon seeing Stephen, I thanked God, and praised him and worshiped him. Normally I would have told Stephen that he needed to tell us when he had to go to the bathroom, but at that moment I was too thankful to correct him and just wanted to thank God that our son was alive. It dawned on me that ten minutes earlier, I was miserable because I didn't like the weather. When my perspective changed, I wouldn't have cared if it rained every day for the rest of my life. The only thing that mattered was that my son was safe.

The right perspective changes everything. When all you can think of is what you want to complain about, you can be pretty miserable and ungrateful. But when you shift your focus, your heart changes. Instead of being poisoned by ingratitude, you're transformed by gratitude and contentment.

ATTITUDES INTO ACTIONS

Take inventory of all God has given you: your life, your health, your talent, your opportunities, your family, your friendships. If you're a Christian, realize you've been saved from your sins, transformed by grace, and filled with God's Spirit. Now it's time to convert any feelings of gratitude into actions.

I'm praying that when nine don't return to offer thanks, you'll be the one who does. You'll worship God, thanking him for who he is and what he's done. You'll be overwhelmed with a heart full of praise. His name will always be on your lips. Gratitude will overflow from your heart.

And as you learn to worship him, content in all things through Christ, your attitude of gratitude will be evident to everyone who comes into contact with you. Even now, I'm certain you know some people who have blessed you, encouraged you, inspired you, or believed in you.

Will you be the one to write the thank-you note to the person who served you or gave you a gift? Will you be the one to express gratitude to a teacher or coach who made a difference in your life? Will you be the one to send an email or a text or to call to express your gratitude to someone who encouraged you or lifted you?

Unlike any other virtue, living with gratitude can change the way you experience your life. Let go of longing for what you don't have, chasing after things that never satisfy you longer than a few minutes. Give God thanks for all that you have. Know that you have everything you need right now. Perhaps no one reminds us of this truth more powerfully than the prophet Isaiah:

Come, all you who are thirsty,
    come to the waters;
and you who have no money,
    come, buy and eat!
Come, buy wine and milk
    without money and without cost.

Why spend money on what is not bread,
   and your labor on what does not satisfy?
Listen, listen to me, and eat what is good,
   and you will delight in the richest of fare.

— Isaiah 55:1 – 2

PART THREE

Sacrificing Self-Justification
for Passionate Obedience

bold behavior

Freedom lies in being bold.
— **Robert Frost**

Until I started high school, I played a variety of sports. You know, some of the manly ones — football, baseball, and soccer. Then toward the end of eighth grade, I suffered an injury that required a lengthy recovery period. So at the beginning of ninth grade, since I was still recovering, I took up tennis, almost as a kind of joke. I knew a cute girl who happened to play tennis, and she provided all the motivation I needed.

Surprisingly enough, though, I made the team and actually started liking the sport. Then, believe it or not, after only four years of playing, I was (barely) good enough to get a scholarship to play for a top-ranked national NAIA school. I was thrilled and expected to do well, but when I stepped on the court at my new college, I realized I was massively outclassed. Hands down, I was by far the worst player on our collegiate team. Also, I happened to be the only

American on an all-Australian team, and this, coupled with my phe-
nomenal losing streak, made me constantly insecure about staying
on the team.

One day I asked the coach, "Why didn't you cut me?"

He hesitated before replying, "Well, honestly, you have the only
car, and I need you to take the players to practice." So that's how I
managed to stay on a college-level team — I had the transportation.

Despite my struggles, I worked really hard and loved competing.
And along the way, I fell into the normal college temptations. As I've
shared before, everything changed on a softball field one night when
I felt so weighed down by my bad choices that I prayed, "God, if you're
there, if this whole Jesus thing is real, please change my life."

When you pray like that, you'd better put on your seat belt,
because sure enough, God did a miraculous work in me and transformed me and made me new in every way. Consequently, I committed to make every area of my life available to God. And one of
those areas was my athletic ability on the tennis court. I knew nothing about being theologically correct, so rather naively, I just prayed,
"God, you've allowed me to be on the tennis team. I'm not very good,
but I'm willing to work harder than ever before. If you make me good
at tennis, I'll tell everybody it was all you."

So that summer I worked harder than ever and trained four to
five hours a day. By the beginning of the fall semester, I came back
determined to make God known through all that I would do, both
on and off the court. At the first match of the year, I knelt down by
the net post and prayed, "God, help me to win. You know I need you;
I'm not any good. Help me be a great witness. I pray that whatever

I do today would make your name well known." Sure enough, that day, I didn't cuss, which was real progress from where I had started. On top of that, I actually won the match. All I could say was, "Thank you, God!"

At the next match, I knelt and prayed again — and won again! My teammates didn't know what to make of my divine transformation on the court. They said things like, "Praying on the court is bold, mate — a little weird, but bold." So I just continued to pray. Believe it or not, by the end of the season, I remained undefeated. I had not lost a single match.

Advancing to the district finals, which was one match away from nationals, I faced a guy named Jeremy, a student from South Africa, who played for Oral Roberts University, a prominent Christian school. The year before, Jeremy had cleaned my clock and beaten me so badly that I wanted to run home crying for my mom. Facing him again in the district finals, I knelt down as always and prayed. When I looked up across the court, my opponent from ORU was praying as well. I was outraged. This was my spiritual routine, not his!

I leaned over and said, "Guess we'll see who has more faith — you or me." And he hollered back, "I'm from ORU; I have more because I'm praying in tongues!"

I shot back, "Well, God just gave me the interpretation of your prayer language, and he says, 'You're going down!'" Despite my rather un-Christlike bragging, God was right and Jeremy went down and I won the title. When I walked over to my teammates, they said, "I can't believe you're undefeated! And you prayed every time! That's really bold, man!"

BOLD AND BEAUTIFUL

Now, my boldness on the tennis court may have been born of naivete as much as inspiration of the Holy Spirit. While my ego may have tried to butt in, I believe God honored the sincerity of my intention to bring him glory through all that I did. As I've matured in my faith, I've learned that God wants us to be bold, to take risks through his leading us out of our comfort zones.

Most of the time, we want to play it safe, to remain comfortable and pursue what's convenient for our busy schedules. But God is bold by his very nature, and as we follow him and are led by his Spirit living within us, we find the strength and courage to take actions that we'd never take on our own.

God wants us to be bold, to take risks through his leading us out of our comfort zones.

We see this illustrated through the vivid descriptions of the struggles and triumphs of the very first group of Christians in the book of Acts. This account was written by Luke, a medical doctor by profession, who captured some of the highlights of the first community of people who believed in Jesus. One of the dominant themes of the book of Acts is the boldness of believers. When you look at the story of the early church, you see miracle after miracle. Relying on nothing but the power of God's Spirit made them undeniably bold in everything they did.

Now, whenever I read these accounts in Acts, I usually ask myself, "Why don't we see these types of miracles in our world today? Or at least in our churches?" Perhaps I'm wrong, but I suspect the answer is because we don't have the same bold faith to act in bold ways to bring about bold results like the early believers did.

Before we go any farther, allow me to define what I mean by boldness. It's not crazy, irrational, odd, illogical, subjective behavior. No, boldness is simply behavior born of belief. Because, as you'll recall, what you believe — about who you are and who God is — determines how you behave. If you believe everybody is going to criticize you, you'll behave cautiously. If you believe you're probably going to fail, you're going to venture out tentatively. If, however, you believe that the one true Lord God is calling you, empowering you, leading you, and equipping you, then you will live boldly. Why? Because boldness is behavior born of belief.

The Greek word from Acts that's translated as boldness is the word *parrhesia*, and this word means more than just skillful speaking. The original Greek word conveys the idea of outspokenness; it means "assurance, courage, and confidence; to act without fear." So often fear keeps our egos front and center and in need of reassurance from other people or from our possessions or titles. But when we lay our egos on the altar of belief, our altar egos become liberated to live by faith and not by fear.

ROCK AND ROLL

Perhaps the boldness spotlight doesn't shine more brightly anywhere in Acts than it does on a guy named Peter. One of Jesus' original twelve disciples, Peter is someone most of us can relate to easily. I know I can. He's the one who's often characterized by bold intentions followed by timid actions. One of the most glaring examples of his bold intentions came right before Jesus was arrested. Peter boldly declared, "If all of these other losers turn their backs on you, I'll still be here. I would never leave you. I'm your guy. I've got your back. I'll never deny you. I'll boldly stand by you."

Before the day ended, not just once but three different times Peter denied knowing Christ. His bold intentions folded under the pressure of having to act in faith. But Peter's story didn't end there; something happened in Peter, and I pray that same something will happen in us. When Jesus died and then rose three days later, Peter encountered his Master with unbounded joy. And Jesus basically said to him, "Hey, you're forgiven; it's all good. Let it go. Shake it off. Be bold. Take care of my sheep. You're my rock" (my slang translation of their conversation, described in John 21).

A switch flipped inside of Peter after that encounter, and suddenly the guy who used to fold his bold under pressure could not be contained. Not long after, he stood before this huge group of people and preached one of the boldest messages in history. He said, "You are a corrupt generation!" Not very politically correct. He said, "You need to turn from your sins, repent in the name of Jesus Christ, and be baptized." And three thousand people were saved on that day. All of a sudden, the New Testament Christian church just exploded, and Peter was bold and on fire and believing God for big things.

For example, he and John were walking along one time when they came across a guy who'd been lame for more than forty years, and they told him to get up and walk. Imagine, in our context, someone who has been in a wheelchair for forty years, and then one day, these two guys come up and say, "In the name of Jesus, take a walk." And he does!

This miraculous healing stirred all kinds of controversy because everybody around knew this guy couldn't walk. And so, some of the temple guards under the command of the Sanhedrin, the religious group in power at that time, sent some people to arrest Peter and John, and they were put on trial in front of the Sanhedrin.

When the Sanhedrin tried someone, all the members of the Sanhedrin, dressed in their official robes, would encircle the defendants to intimidate them. They would hurl questions from all directions and then decide on the defendants' fate, typically saying, "We're just going to beat you," or, "We're going to imprison you," or, "We're going to kill you." So it wasn't looking good for these two followers of Jesus.

In the middle of this ominous gathering, Peter and John were asked, "By what name and by what authority do you do these things?"

Were they tongue-tied or intimidated?

See for yourself: "Then Peter, filled with the Holy Spirit, said to them, 'Rulers and elders of our people, are we being questioned today because we've done a good deed for a crippled man? Do you want to know how he was healed? Let me clearly state to all of you and to all the people of Israel that he was healed by the powerful name of Jesus Christ the Nazarene,...'" Then Peter delivered the perfect strike to make sure they got the point: "'... the man you crucified but whom God raised from the dead'" (Acts 4:8 – 10 NLT).

WHAT'S IN A NAME?

Now, I cannot possibly overstate how bold that was. The Sanhedrin hated Jesus, were glad he was gone, and hoped never to hear from him again. And the foundation of their convictions was the belief that resurrecting the dead is impossible. So Peter pointed right at the people who used their power to kill Jesus and said, "Where did I get this kind of power to heal a guy who's been crippled for forty years? You remember Jesus, don't you? The innocent man you set up and crucified. Well, he's back from the dead." Essentially, Peter's response was like a declaration of war, the last thing these Jewish religious leaders wanted to hear.

Now, what's really interesting is that two thousand years ago, what name was so controversial? The name of Jesus, right? Two thousand years later, what name brings so much controversy? The name of Jesus. Think about it. In our world today, you can be spiritually bold about all sorts of things and it's fine. Everybody tolerates a little God talk, a little spirituality talk. It's just when you bring Jesus into it that everybody gets all freaked out. Let's be honest, you can go on *Oprah* and talk about a higher power all day long. "Oh, yeah, that's good, that's interesting. Oh, and God did this, and the Spirit did this, and I'm a spiritual person. I've got spirituality." Oh yeah, huggie, huggie, sniff, sniff! But as soon as you say, "Jesus," everything changes, doesn't it?

I was asked to pray at a professional sporting event. The sponsors said, "You can pray whatever you want." I smiled and said, "Anything I want?" They said, "Yes, anything you want. Well, anything you want as long as it doesn't violate our one rule. You cannot pray in the name of Jesus."

Without missing a beat, I said, "What name do I pray in?"

They were agitated now. "We don't know. You can pray in whatever name you want to. You can pray in the Creator's name, in God's name, in the Lord's name, in the Big Guy's name, in your name, or your momma's name, but you can't pray in the name of Jesus."

Why? Because there's something about that name. The name of Jesus carries supernatural authority that empowers us in ways we can't even grasp. So when Peter and John cite Jesus as their power source, the religious leaders couldn't believe what they were seeing: "The members of the council were amazed when they saw the boldness of Peter and John, for they could see that they were ordinary men with no special training in the Scriptures. They also recognized them as men who had been with Jesus" (Acts 4:13 NLT).

IDIOT'S GUIDE TO BOLDNESS

The Jewish religious leaders were stunned to see such audacity from a couple of regular Joes like John and Peter. It'd be like you and me standing before the Supreme Court telling them that we know what's best for the country's judicial system. They'd look at us, aware that we're not attorneys or scholars trained in the courtroom (work with me if you happen to be an attorney or trained in the courtroom), and wonder what makes us think we are so knowledgeable and confident.

But here's the thing: God gives ordinary people extraordinary boldness. You don't have to be an expert or a scholar, have a seminary degree or experience as a missionary to serve Christ with amazing power. Consider the language of the verse again: "[The leaders] could see that [Peter and John] were ordinary men with no special training in the Scriptures." Now, the Greek word translated as "ordinary" is the word *idiotas*. This word can mean unlearned; it can mean unschooled; it can mean ordinary. But the literal translation for the word *idiotas* is — you guessed it — "idiot"! Don't you love it?

Sometimes I think the Bible translators are just too polite. A literal translation renders this verse as "these guys were amazed and couldn't believe the boldness of these idiots." There's no mean-spirited name-calling here; it's just a fact that these guys had no special training or religious education that qualified them to heal a lame man. Here's the deal: if you're the best of the best, the brightest of the brightest, God obviously will use you for his kingdom. It's just that he specializes in using idiots — normal, everyday people like you and me. He loves, absolutely loves, using ordinary people.

> God gives ordinary people extraordinary boldness.

Our God loves to take people that others overlook and give them boldness. You may be thinking, "Well, I'm a Christian, but I'm just not naturally bold. I'm kind of a quiet person. I'm not a seminary guy. I'm not a natural leader or teacher of the Bible. You know, I'm just a stay-at-home mom." Or, "I'm just a student." Or, "I'm just a dude, man!" Remember, there are so many different ways to be bold, so many unique, exceptional ways to be bold for Christ.

You may be in your workplace and everybody is gossiping. "Hey, have you heard the latest?" And you look at them and say, "You know what? Because of my faith, I'm not going to be a part of this." And you walk off. That's boldness in action.

You may be a teenager or a young woman, and you love God and want to please him. All of your friends — well, let's be honest, they dress like prostitutes. I'm not trying to sound like your dad or some-one who's totally out of it, but you know what I'm talking about. Your friends want to go clubbing, and they're trying to see how tight and skimpy they can wear their clothes without hurting themselves. And you refuse to go along and dress like that. You say, "I'm going to be modest to honor God, and they can think what they want about me." You are *bold* for Christ.

Maybe you're a single guy and all your buddies are bar-hopping and chasing women, trying to score that night's conquest. And you stand up to them and say, "You know what? I'm not going to treat women like they're objects. I'm actually going to treat them like they're created in the image of God. And I'm going to honor my future wife, whom I've not met yet, and honor my God, who calls me to different standards. And I'm not going to do that!"

You may be in a business deal you could make a lot of money on, but you're looking at the situation and realizing, "I don't feel right about this. I don't think it's really ethical." And you walk away from a very profitable business deal because of your faith. What were you? You were *bold*.

NEVER TOO BOLD

When you become spiritually bold for the glory of God, your bold-ness will amaze the world. We're told that the members of the Sanhe-drin were amazed at the boldness of Peter and John. Why? Because they knew they could kill these guys, and these guys didn't care. They were "wow, we don't have a category for this" crazy amazed. Even if the council members didn't believe what these two idiots were saying, it was clear that Peter and John had no doubt whatsoever about their faith in Christ.

Speaking with this kind of boldness before a hostile audience is not something most of us have ever experienced. But each of us faces opportunities to be bold scaled to our life circumstances. I told you about the year that I managed to go undefeated. Well, at the end of the year, they had this awards ceremony for all of the sports, the big sporting awards ceremony. I had just met Amy, and we were invited to go. I knew I'd be getting an award because my parents were invited, and so I thought, "I'm getting something!" I had no idea that they actually were going to give me the most prestigious honor awarded, the Athlete of the Year.

When they made the presentation, I walked to the podium to receive my award, and the presenter said, "Craig, is there anything you'd like to say?" And I remembered my prayer almost a year prior: "God, if you make me better, I'll tell everybody about you."

So I grabbed the microphone, and I preached my first sermon. It had like seventy-three points and I probably rambled quite a bit. But it didn't matter, because my heart was open and God shone through. It was church good. It was so good they should have taken up an offering.

I went on and on and started to cry about who I was as a sinful person and what God had done. I talked about everything — which wasn't much at that point in my life — that I knew about God and his goodness. And as I closed my little impromptu sermon and tried to regain my composure, I thought, "I'll never have a friend again." So imagine how shocked I was when everyone in the banquet room gave me a standing ovation.

I'll never forget that as I made my way back to my seat, I walked by a guy who put out his hand to shake mine. He played a different sport, and I didn't know him well, but we'd been at parties together and had many mutual friends. He stuck out his hand and said, "That's the boldest thing that I've ever seen in my entire life." I thanked him, well aware of how fast my heart was still beating in my chest.

> When you become spiritually bold for the glory of God, your boldness will amaze the world.

Here's what I want to ask you: When was the last time someone was amazed by your boldness? When was the last time you stopped someone in their tracks because they were undone by your bold speech and actions? Now, keep in mind, I'm not talking about a wacky, odd, cheesy, thirty-three-bumper-stickers-on-your-SUV kind of Christian drive-by witness. I'm not talking about being bold in a bad-Christian-television way to make people dislike you or ridicule you. I'm talking about being bold with integrity. The kind of boldness where you're serving people faithfully in Jesus' name, where you're encouraging them, where you're living in a way that reflects Christ's compassion and selflessness, where others look at you and say, "There's something different about this person." The kind of boldness where you're so generous with your money and your heart and your time, where you've served your way into people's lives, and therefore you've earned the right to say, "I really do love you; may I tell you about my God?"

WAKE-UP CALL

You may be reading this and cringing, thinking, "But I'm just not that kind of person. Does God really want me to act bold just to prove I'm a Christian?" Which leads us to a very important point. Spiritual boldness is not our goal; knowing Christ is our goal. Boldness is merely a byproduct of following Jesus and living as he lived, showing others the love of the Father. Spiritual boldness comes from knowing Christ.

Remember our friends Peter and John and their bold stand before the Sanhedrin? We're told that the council members were amazed because these were ordinary guys, but we're also told that they recognized these guys as men who had been with Jesus. How in the world could Peter stand in the face of possible death and declare what he did? He knew Jesus. He could be bold because he had been with Jesus. Here's the key: you have to remember this: boldness is not the point; knowing Jesus is the point.

> Spiritual boldness comes from knowing Christ.

When you live a life of faith, when you're directed by the Spirit, you're going to see opportunity after opportunity to be bold. Why? Because you've had time with Jesus. As your faith grows, so does your boldness. As your boldness grows, it leads to results. When you see spiritual results, guess what? You spend more time with Jesus, and when you spend more time with Jesus, guess what? You get more faith, and you start praying bigger prayers and you see God work, which leads to boldness, which then leads to the Acts-type of results, which leads to more time with Jesus. And it goes on and on and on.

The problem is that the opposite is true as well. When you don't spend time with Jesus, you don't have much faith, so you're not bold. So you don't see results, and you don't want to spend much time with him, and then, well, you guessed it. You end up living for the lower things of this world, wondering why you're empty the whole time. You end up letting your ego lead you instead of sacrificing it in pursuit of the altar ego that only Christ wants to give you.

There's so much more God wants to use you to do to make a difference in this world. You're here for a purpose, and God wants to stir you up. Consider this a bold wake-up call.

Remember the guy I told you about at the awards ceremony? He wasn't a Christian, but he shook my hand and said that it was the boldest thing he'd ever seen. Well, I hadn't seen that guy for years until recently when I bumped into him. I said, "Hey, you're the guy from back in school! How's it going?"

He said, "Yeah, it's great to see you! I'm doing well."

I looked down and he was wearing a WEIRD bracelet that was part of a series our church had just completed. I couldn't believe my eyes! I said, "Are you weird?"

And he said, "Because normal isn't working!"

We both laughed, and I said, "No way! What's up with that?"

He said, "Man, Groeschel, I remember back in school when you gave that bold speech at the awards dinner. I wanted to believe you were different because I knew how you were, but honestly I thought it was going to wear off. I thought it was just a religious thing you were going through."

He paused before continuing. "Yeah, we all thought it would wear off. Years and years went by, and somebody invited me to LifeChurch. When I walked in and saw you up there, I freaked. Here I was all these years later, and I heard you saying the same thing in the same way, and I realized it hadn't worn off. Jesus had truly changed you, and because he changed you, I wanted him to change me."

Jesus loves you and me enough to change us and use us to show others what he can do. I'm telling you, you can make a difference like that if you'll spend time with Jesus. He'll grow your faith and give you boldness, and you'll see results that will blow your mind. I challenge you in the boldest way possible to be the real deal. Refuse to be a halfhearted, lukewarm Christian. Fall so in love with God that everywhere you go, you overflow with a spiritual boldness of love and compassion that draws people to the joy of life in Christ.

bold prayers

To be a Christian without prayer
is no more possible
than to be alive without breathing.

— Martin Luther King Jr.

If you ever met my mom, it wouldn't take you long to recognize that she is an amazing lady who isn't afraid to say what's on her mind. I like to think of it as the spiritual gift of spunk. She was in the hospital a number of years ago and about to go into surgery. I had come to be with her and reassure her and could tell that she was nervous. I could tell she was relieved when, a few minutes before it was time to roll her to the operating room, a hospital chaplain stopped by and asked if she would like him to pray with her.

Mom said, "I'm so glad you're here! Yes, please pray with me."

The chaplain said, "What's your religious preference?"

"Christian," my mom said.

"What denomination?" the chaplain asked.

And she said, "Well, I really don't have a denomination. I'm just a Christian."

The chaplain remained calm and said, "In order to pray with you, I need to know your specific denomination. What kind of church did you grow up in?"

Mom and I were both a little bit confused. She said, "I grew up in the Methodist Church."

The chaplain looked pleased to have an answer and said, "Great! Give me one second." And he whipped out his little prayer book, turned to the table of contents, and found the appropriate Methodist prayer. He flipped to the page the prayer was on and started reading, "Dear God, I pray for — "

"Wait, wait, wait!" Mom interrupted. "Would somebody please get this guy out of here and get me someone who knows how to pray their own prayers?"

I might've been embarrassed if I hadn't been so busy laughing.

WORD MIRRORS

Now, there's nothing wrong with praying a traditional prayer printed in a book and deemed appropriate for Methodists (or Baptists or whomever). But I believe my mom's reaction was ignited by her understanding of prayer as personal, conversational, sincere language from a person's heart to God's ear. Since that incident with Mom, I've learned that prayers are indeed the lifeblood of a believer's faith.

I've also learned that there's no better mirror for someone's theology than the content of their prayers. What you pray for reflects what you believe about God. What you pray for, or what you don't pray for, reflects what you believe about who God is, what his character is like, and his disposition toward us, his children.

It's as if the words we use in our prayers are like pieces of mirrored glass, each one reflecting our beliefs about the one we're addressing.

> **What you pray for reflects what you believe about God.**

For example, if you don't pray at all, then you likely don't believe in God or don't believe he answers prayer. If you pray very small prayers all of the time, you probably don't really believe in a God who answers big prayers. If almost all of your prayers are for yourself and your own well-being — "bless me, help me, comfort me, be with me" — then this reflects your belief that God is there to serve you. People who hold this belief, whether they admit it or not, often end up getting angry and disgruntled if God doesn't give them what they asked for.

The specific language we use when we pray says a lot about what we believe about God as well. For example, when someone is facing a tough situation and they exhaust all possibilities of resolving the problem themselves, they say, "Well, now all we can do is pray!" If prayer for you is a last resort, this reflects what you believe about God.

Can't you just see God up in heaven saying, "So you're down to prayer now? You mean it's all up to me? Well, no pressure! Thanks a lot for waiting until the last minute, like I don't have a trillion other prayers to answer before breakfast." I'm not trying to be irreverent here; I'm only trying to illustrate that what you say when you pray clearly reflects what you believe about God.

Take a moment right now and think back over what you prayed last week. If your first thought is, "Well, I don't think I really prayed for anything last week," then I think that speaks for itself. If you can't really remember what you prayed for, what does that say about your belief in God? Is he just as forgettable?

Maybe you're saying, "Oh yeah, I prayed last week. I prayed for this, and then for that, and then some more of this and some of that." As you think through what and who you prayed for last week, I encourage you to jot down at least three or four of your requests. Now, as you look over your prayer list, ask yourself this question: if God answered yes to all of your prayers last week, if he just miraculously granted everything you prayed, what would be different in the world today?

Think about it. If God answered everything that you prayed for last week, what would be different in the world today? Chances are pretty good that if you prayed like most people in our culture, the only things that would be different would be in your immediate surroundings.

For example, if you're a single lady and you prayed last week about your wanting to get married, then God would have given you a handsome, on-fire Christian who prays for you. Or at least a cute, churchgoing boyfriend. Or if you're married and you prayed for your husband to be a spiritual leader, wow — now he's like the Billy Graham of your neighborhood.

Or depending on your particular request, your wife would be more responsive, or you got the raise at work, or you qualified for the loan on the house you want, or your grandma was healed of cancer, or your friend's marriage that's on the rocks is now rock solid.

For years that's how I prayed. I really learned from Amy, my wife, to pray really big prayers, because I'm telling you, if God answered every one of the prayers she prayed last week, churches would be overflowing today with new believers, because she prays for evangelism around the world every single day. She prays for revival to break out in churches. She prays for orphans to be adopted by the thousands. She prays for those trapped in human trafficking to be set free. She prays for addicts to find the only thing that can ever satisfy them. Amy prays really, really big prayers, and I've learned so much just by watching her.

No matter what we prayed for last week, I'm convinced that if we really want to make a big difference in this life, we must learn to pray some very bold prayers.

PRAY LIKE YOU MEAN IT

You'll recall that in the last chapter, we looked at the vibrant picture of the early Christian church that's described for us in the book of Acts. We saw how Peter and John were preaching and teaching and healing, all in the name of Jesus, and seeing unbelievable results. Peter preached boldly and called a group of people a corrupt generation, then told them to repent and be baptized in the name of Jesus. And miraculously, three thousand people were born into the family of God. Then, Peter and John traveled along and, at a gate called Beautiful outside the temple, came across a guy who had been lame for forty years. And they boldly said, "Pick up your mat, walk." And he did.

The Jewish religious leaders, in a council called the Sanhedrin, were disturbed because these guys were outside the box of the religious merit system they controlled. Consequently, they arrested Peter and John, put them on trial, and asked, "Where did you get this kind of power and authority? By what name are you doing these things?"

In a move as bold as it gets, Peter and John said, "Let us state clearly, we are doing this in the name of Jesus Christ, the man that you crucified, but whom God raised from the dead."

The religious leaders would have loved to keep them in prison, or perhaps even kill them for what they were doing. But because the lame man had been healed, they couldn't risk a public riot since so many had seen the miracle. Against their wishes, they had to release Peter and John.

This is where we pick up our lesson in boldness. "On their release, Peter and John went back to their own people and reported all that the chief priests and the elders had said to them. When they heard this, they raised their voices together in prayer to God. 'Sovereign Lord,' they said, 'you made the heavens and the earth and the sea, and everything in them.... Now, Lord, consider their threats and enable your servants to speak your word with great boldness.' ... After they prayed, the place where they were meeting was shaken. And they were all filled with the Holy Spirit and spoke the word of God boldly" (Acts 4:23 – 24, 29, 31).

If they had been fearful, Peter and John could've returned to home base and reported, "Whew, that was a close one! They threatened us, so we can never speak in Jesus' name again." No, instead, their response was like a high-octane, old-fashioned revival service.

"When they heard this, they raised their voices together in prayer to God." Wow, I love this response! There's something incredibly powerful when believers come together, especially in the face of adversity, and lift up their hearts in prayer to God.

Now, I'll be honest — I'm never the guy who lines up first for the seven-hour prayer meeting. I'm sorry, but as much as I love God and love other people, I just don't like getting in there and holding hands and crying and blowing noses and holding hands some more and praying for hours on end. Call me shallow if you will, but it just makes me uncomfortable.

Take the whole hand-holding thing. You've got people on both sides, and you never know proper hand-holding etiquette. You're over with one guy and under with another, and then you're trying to figure out, intertwined or cupped? Let's be honest; it's downright awkward.

Then, inevitably, you've got unequally yoked hand partners. You've got the dead-fish guy that's just, you know, soft and lifeless — come on, dude, wake up and give me something. And then you've got the hard gripper who squeezes tighter the louder they pray until you lose all sensation up to your elbow. Finally, just to be clear: At the end of the group prayer when someone finally closes with "in Jesus' name, amen," just a quick little squeeze and let go. Don't you dare keep holding hands after everyone's opened their eyes — very weird, and not in a good way.

Even though it may not feel totally natural, there's something incredible about praying with someone else. I may not have a lot of faith, but when I hear someone else praying, it's almost like I get to climb up on top of their faith, and then I pray and it builds my faith, and it's like we have this cumulative, exponential faith together. We read in Scripture that there's power when believers come together in agreement before God. And this is exactly what these believers were experiencing. Under extraordinary persecution, they came together as one voice and prayed boldly to their Father.

They begin by addressing him as "Sovereign Lord," signaling their awareness of his power and authority not just over them but over the Sanhedrin, the city, the whole world, and beyond. It's not as if God needed them to remind him that he's in charge. No, these believers were putting themselves in the right position of worship to a holy God. It's almost as if they were reminding themselves, "God, you are Supreme over all."

Then they pray one of the boldest requests ever uttered: We're going to pray for boldness. We are going to ask God to make us bolder. In their prayer, they refer to threats, and we don't know specifically which threats they're talking about. We can only assume it was the threats of being beaten, put in prison, and killed. But instead of praying for protection and safety and a strong defense against their persecutors, these guys prayed, "Lord, enable your servants to speak your word with great boldness."

Now, if I'm looking on as an objective bystander, I'm likely thinking, "Isn't boldness what got you arrested the first time?" I mean, how much bolder can you be, right? If it were up to me, I'd advise them to lay low with the whole Jesus thing for a while. Let things cool down and then take it nice and easy and see who's friendly and who's not.

Good thing it wasn't up to me.

LOWER PRICES, BOLDER PRAYERS

Let me ask you: have you ever prayed for God to make *you* bolder? For most of us, myself included, this is a radical, others-centered prayer. Boldness typically doesn't help me or make my life easier. It usually only requires more from me than I'm comfortable giving. Boldness is for the benefit of someone else, to help them know the love of God through Jesus Christ. When we're used to praying mostly egocentric, self-focused prayers, it can be very unsettling to pray for boldness. And yet, if we are to live from our truest identity in Christ, then we must lay our egos on the altar of his boldness.

Maybe you've heard the old saying, "Be careful what you wish for; you might get it." I think the same is true when we pray bold prayers. Recently, I experienced this firsthand as I've continued to try to live out my boldness. I had been praying every day for several weeks that God would make me bold, only to see results in a most unexpected place.

Amy and I used to go on exciting dates, but with six kids and all of our responsibilities, our date-night destination is now the grocery store. Don't feel sorry for us. It's still romantic; we even make out in the frozen food aisle sometimes! So one Friday night recently, we went to our local Walmart, and I discovered a new kind of love I've never known before. It's called Triple Double-Stuf Oreo cookies. Who knew such bliss existed? Glory

> **Boldness is for the benefit of someone else, to help them know the love of God through Jesus Christ.**

to God! I didn't even know such a creation was possible. But then, I should have, because with God, all things are possible — even triple double-stuf!

So I'm in Walmart, discreetly sneaking a bag of my new most beloved cookie into the bottom of our cart, when I look up and see this guy coming toward me. Amy's still distracted looking for healthy treats (which is an oxymoron, I keep telling her), so I smile and try to look friendly. He says, "Pastor Craig! I'm from the South Tulsa Campus of LifeChurch! Man, am I glad to see you!"

So we stood there talking for a while, and then he lowered his voice and leaned in. "I've got to be real honest with you. I'm struggling with an addiction to pornography, and I hate it, but I can't stop. Would you mind praying for me?"

I said, "Of course, I'll pray for you." Now usually when I say this, it means, I'll pray for you later, but without even thinking about it, I blurted out, "You want to pray right now?"

"Here? In Walmart?" And he kind of looked at me funny.

I shrugged and said, "I'll pray if you want me to."

His face broke into a huge grin and he said, "Let's pray!"

And so I just kind of put my hand on his shoulder, because I'm not holding hands with another man in Walmart even if we are praying, and I prayed for him and kept my voice low and just asked God to give him the victory in Christ that is already his. No exorcism or dramatic televangelist theatrics. You know, just a sincere, bold request before God.

Now, as I'm winding up my prayer, I sort of looked up and peeked — which is legal because Scripture says to "watch and pray."

And I saw this other couple come up and stand right beside us. Seemed a bit odd, but who am I to call someone weird while I stand praying in Walmart? So I wrapped up my prayer and shook my new buddy's hand and told him to be free and stay strong.

As he walked away, this couple immediately came up to me and said, "Pastor Craig, we noticed you praying just now. Would you be willing to pray for us too? Our marriage is really struggling."

I said, "Absolutely!"

We started praying, and then, with God as my witness, another lady walked up and hovered near us, clearly waiting her turn. I finished my prayer for the couple and wished them well, and then, turning to the lady, I said, "Come on up! What campus do you go to?"

She looked at me funny and said, "What's a campus?"

"Aren't you from LifeChurch?" I said.

"What's LifeChurch? I just saw you praying and wondered if you'd pray for me."

I broke out in a big smile and said, "Absolutely! Let's just pray."

I'm telling you, if you pray for boldness, you'd better be careful or you'll wind up praying by the cat food in Walmart. In fact, I dare you, I double-dog dare you, I Triple-Double-Stuf-Oreo dare you. I dare you to ask God to use you in other people's lives today. Pray, "Lord, use me today, use me for your glory, make me bold, stir me up, give me eyes to see the needs of those I work with, give me a heart sensitive to those who are hurting, give me a prompting of the Spirit to minister to those who are around me." You pray and you watch as God will do something in you, and that stirs you up with boldness for his glory.

BIGGER, BETTER, BOLDER

God wants to use us in more places than just our local Walmart. I believe he delights in using us to facilitate his power in seemingly impossible situations. If we return to the example of Peter and John and the early believers in the book of Acts, we see that they not only prayed for boldness. They prayed for the power to perform miracles: "Stretch out your hand to heal and perform signs and wonders through the name of your holy servant Jesus" (Acts 4:30).

They're praying big, bold prayers — heal-the-sick, raise-the-dead, preach-before-thousands kind of prayers. You want to make a big and bold difference in this world? Then pray big, bold prayers. Remember, what you pray for reflects what you believe about God. If you pray small prayers, then you're believing in a small God.

My fear is that most of the time, most of us pray small prayers. "Dear God, thank you for this day. Thank you for this day. Thank you for this day." I wonder if God ever thinks, "You've thanked me for each day the last forty-three years. I got it already!" Or how many times do we pray, "God be with us; Lord be with us"? God's like, "I already promised you I would, so I will. I'll never leave you. I'll never forsake you. Done deal." Or, "Give us traveling mercies today." Which always makes me wonder if God thinks, "Put on your seat belt, drive the speed limit, chances are pretty good you'll make it there safely." Instead, I believe God wants us to ask him for the impossible:

> You want to make a big and bold difference in this world? Then pray big, bold prayers.

"Ask me something hard! Give me something that's so big that when it happens, everybody's going to know I did it."

Years ago, my pastor, Nick Harris, was teaching us in a staff Bible study about praying for big things. After hearing him one week, I went off to teach at this youth camp, all fired up from Nick's teaching, ready to do my own bold teaching. The camp was filled with a good group of earnest Christian kids, along with some curious seekers. However, there was this one guy who obviously didn't believe anything I said. He had his hands in his pockets, slumped in his chair, sullen the whole time, an angry scowl about to erupt on his face.

After I finished teaching, this kid came up to me and said, "I don't get it, I don't believe it, I'm not buying it, and I'm out of here." He wanted to make sure I knew how he really felt.

I said, "Hang on, hang on, hang on! Let's talk. I understand you don't get it, but let's just talk about it. You're obviously hurting. What's going on?"

He started opening up and shared that he had a lot of painful issues with his dad. The more I listened, the more I sensed that God wanted me to pray for him, so I asked if he minded.

He said, "You can pray, but it's not going to do any good. Lots of people have prayed for me, and nothing has changed."

I said, "That's fine." And my mind and heart were racing. I was doing a double prayer. (You can do that when you're a pastor.) Just as I was about to pray for him, I silently prayed, "God, what do I say?"

In that moment, I felt compelled by God to do something that I'd never done before and that I've never done since. It's the only time in my whole life I've ever done this. I looked at this kid and prayed,

"God, I ask you in the name of your Son Jesus to reveal yourself to him now."

When I finished praying, the kid opened his eyes, and he just started shaking. I'm not kidding. He looked at me and said, "I think God is on me! I think God is on me!"

I took a big step back because I didn't know what was about to go down. This kid, who only seconds before didn't believe in God, just crumbled and fell to the ground and kept crying out, "God is on me!" I knelt down and put my arm around him, and there was crying and there was praying, and when he stood up, he was a different young man. He was different because someone believed that God could do what God said.

Pray bold prayers, pray bold prayers, pray bold prayers. Pray. Bold. Prayers.

You say, "Well, what if it doesn't happen? Why do so many people not pray bold prayers?"

Keeping in mind that our prayers reflect our belief in God, I believe some people think, "Well, I don't want to be disappointed if I ask God for something and he doesn't give it to me." Others say, "I tried before; it didn't work." Or, I love this one, "I don't want to make God look bad." So we give God these little escapes, like "if it be thy will" or "according to your purposes."

Let me tell you, here's where I am, and I mean this as sincerely and seriously as I can express it. I have no fear anytime, anywhere asking God for anything, because I have seen him do things that are inexplicable in human terms. Now, does this mean God always does it? No! No! No, of course not. In the Old Testament, we see Joshua prayed and the sun stood still. But sometimes you pray for the sun to stand still, and the sun sets. I'm convinced, though, that the same boldness that's required to ask God for big things can handle it if he says no. My faith in God is big enough that I can ask him for anything, and my faith can handle God's saying no. My faith can handle it because he is the Sovereign God; he's in charge; he knows.

SHOWING UP AND SHOWING OFF

There's a wonderful couple in our church, Kevin and Amanda. At the age of twenty-nine, Kevin had a brain aneurysm rupture, which usually results in immediate death. Only he lived. No one in our local medical community would operate on him; there were only two doctors in our country who would. So Kevin traveled to San Francisco for brain surgery.

They operated on him, and then he spent the next month in ICU. It took him more than a year to learn to talk, walk, and eat on his own. He went on to have a normal, healthy life. But several years later, they found another aneurysm. You can only imagine how devastating this must've been. But here's the amazing part of their story. Kevin and Amanda, their friends and church family, we all prayed the boldest prayer we knew to pray — for God to take away this aneurysm and heal Kevin completely. And that's what God did! His doctors were beside themselves and saw no scientific reason for its disappearance, and yet it was unmistakably gone.

God showed up and God showed off. And he's going to get all of the glory. If God doesn't answer our prayers the way we think he should, he is still God, and it doesn't shake our faith, because we believe he is the sovereign Creator of the universe, and we are going to pray bold prayers, because what we pray for reflects what we believe about our good God.

Pray for miracles. Don't be a Christian in name only, but be filled with faith that all things are possible with our God. Be bolder than you could ever imagine. Pray the impossible. It's so easy to pray soft, safe, sterile prayers. But when we crucify our doubts and live in the security of who God is, we can't help but pray bold prayers. Our altar ego builds a bold faith in an amazingly audacious God.

Father, I ask that in your presence, you would stir me to real, deep, and growing faith in you. You know me too well. I kind of pray smaller prayers, or more self-centered prayers, and I really want to pray some bold prayers. I want to believe you for big things. I want what I pray for to reflect what I believe about you. And I want to live in the truth that you are all-powerful, ever-present, all-knowing. I truly believe that all things are possible with you. I ask for boldness so that I may make a bold difference for your kingdom. In the name of your Son, amen.

Pat Murphy

Product Line Manager

bold words

Say what you need to say.

— John Mayer

I happen to live in an area of the country where there are lots of poisonous snakes, especially copperheads. Now, if you know anything about me, then you know that I passionately hate, hate, hate, *hate* poisonous snakes. I hate the way they go slithering and sneaking around in the bushes, hiding under rocks, and sunning next to a creek or lakeshore like they're on vacation. I hate everything about them. I don't just hate them because they're sneaky, vile, evil, and deceptive; I hate them because they're dangerous. My neighbor got bitten and his leg swelled up to the size of his waist, and boy, was it nasty. I've seen countless pets and livestock slain by snakes' deadly poison as well, including one of our favorite family pets, and I do not intend to let that happen to my wife or one of my kids.

So every year, I kill several copperheads when they come close to my house or my kids. Whenever I see a wriggling, slithering band of emerald-brown-gold, I take a shovel and with the power of the Holy Spirit in me, I chop off the snake's head. Then I take the rest of its body and hang it in a tree in our yard. They can't say I didn't warn them, because I send a very clear message to all the other snakes: Groeschel means business! If I made a snakeskin wallet or belt every time I killed one, I could open a kiosk at the mall.

Occasionally I'll take a picture and tweet it or put it on my Facebook page just in case there are any tech-savvy snakes out there. Usually the response, though, is from some of you softer, more politically correct naturalists out there who shout back at me that I shouldn't be killing snakes because they're one of God's creations, because they balance the environment by killing rodents, blah, blah, hiss, hiss. Keep in mind, though, when you send such a message reminding me that we live in such a pathetic, politically correct world where we don't want to hurt a poisonous snake that could bite my eight-year-old, that next time I'll just bag them up and take them to your house so you can love and nurture them.

SILENCE IS DEADLY

This mindset of never offending anyone anywhere has overflowed into the church as well. More and more, I hear Christians say things like, "You know, I don't want to upset anybody, so I try not to speak too boldly about my faith." Consequently, a common mindset in the church today is that to be good witnesses, we need to just let our actions speak for us. Don't get me wrong, this is a great place to start, because hands down, we do want our lives to reflect Christ. But there are times when we can't just let our lives speak for us; we must use our words to witness boldly as well.

Think of it this way. If you come over to my house, and we decide to go for a little walk outside, and suddenly I see a copperhead (their defense is to blend in, and my eyes are trained skillfully to see them, while you probably are not looking for one), I have a choice. If there's a snake in the grass right at the edge of our path, I can simply walk a few steps away from that spot. In this way, I let my actions be a witness to you; if you're paying attention, maybe you'll veer toward me and away from the snake.

But you might not notice, and if you step on the snake, you're going to be very miserable and probably not come back to my house again. Rather than just letting my life be a witness, a more loving response in this instance would be to shout, "Snake!" You need to hear bold words in that moment to avoid danger. Then, of course, we could take a shovel and behead him together, hang his lifeless body on a tree, and post a picture on our Facebook pages.

Yes, there is a time to let your life be a witness. There are also times when you have to speak boldly to keep people out of harm's way and lead them into a better way of life.

As we explore what it means to sacrifice our egos in order to live from our altar egos, we've seen that our true nature is to act boldly since boldness is behavior born out of a belief. Similarly, I'm convinced that we speak boldly about what we believe deeply. Returning to the early church, time and time again we see Christians not only behaving boldly but speaking boldly as well. After Saul, the persecutor of Jesus' disciples, became Paul, the apostle to all people, we're told that Saul "moved about freely in Jerusalem, speaking boldly in the name of the Lord" (Acts 9:28).

> We speak boldly about what we believe deeply.

After Saul joined up with his pal Barnabas, they continued doing more of the same. "Paul and Barnabas spent considerable time there, speaking boldly for the Lord" (Acts 14:3). And as we saw in the previous chapter, as believers faced extraordinary persecution for their beliefs, they prayed for even more boldness. As a result, "they were all filled with the Holy Spirit and spoke the word of God boldly" (Acts 4:31).

Why? Because we speak boldly about what we believe deeply.

SEEING IS BELIEVING

When we behave boldly and speak boldly as the result of bold prayers, then God's involvement is undeniable. Even the Jewish leaders in the Sanhedrin who wanted to trap Peter and John for healing in the name of Jesus couldn't deny that something miraculous had happened. They were cornered by public awareness that the man who had been lame for forty years was now doing the Electric Slide. Since they couldn't deny the miracle, but were opposed to increasing any interest in Jesus and his supposed resurrection, the leaders were beside themselves over what to do with Peter and John. "'What are we going to do with these men?' they asked. 'Everyone living in Jerusalem knows they have performed a notable sign, and we cannot deny it'" (Acts 4:16).

Don't you love it? Essentially, they were saying, "We don't believe it, but we can't deny it. We don't understand it, but we can't ignore it."

I love it when God does something that's so obviously supernatural that the world has no choice but to look on and say, "We don't really believe it and we don't understand it, but, boy, we cannot deny it."

I confess that as much as I try to remain aware of God's powerful presence in any situation, sometimes my rational, ego-driven doubt gets in the way. I remember when my oldest daughter, Catie, was three or four years old, and she got into poison ivy and became covered from head to toe with this horrible, red, itchy rash. We took her to the doctor, and he said it was one of the worst cases of poison ivy he'd seen. He gave us some special ointment to treat it, but said, "It's going to be several days of nothing but pain for her, so just brace yourselves."

When we got home, little Catie said, "Well, I'm going to pray and ask Jesus to heal me. I don't want to wait all week long."

Being the great man of faith that I am, I said, "Oh, baby, you are so cute. What a sweet idea. But you heard what the doctor said."

She looked at me funny and put her hands on her hips. "Daddy, I don't care what the doctor said. I'm going to pray!" She closed her eyes and folded her hands and said, "Jesus, I just ask that you heal me by morning."

Her father the pastor said, "Now, Catie, it may not happen. So don't be disappointed if, you know …" And basically I tried to talk her out of her faith, even as I thought I was protecting her from her naivete.

She just smiled at me and ran off to play.

The next morning, Amy and I were sound asleep when Catie came bouncing into our room at 5:00 a.m. and turned on all the lights.

"Honey, what're you doing?" I said.

We squinted through sleepy eyes and saw that she'd stripped off her pajamas and wore nothing but her Barney panties. Jumping on the edge of our bed, she bounced a couple of times and said, "Mom and Dad — tada!"

I was trying to remember what day it was and to figure out what in the world Catie was talking about. Amy rolled over and said, "What are you doing? Turn off the lights, naked girl!"

Catie jumped higher and said louder. "No, no, no! Tada!"

And that's when Amy and I both realized it at the same time. The rash that had covered her was gone. My first thought was, "I don't believe it, but I can't deny it. It was there, she prayed, and now it's gone."

Maybe you've experienced something similar in your life. Others looked on and said, "We don't understand it, we don't even want to fully believe it, but we can't deny it. Something's changed." Maybe you were struggling in your marriage, and then your husband met up with Jesus in a radical moment, and now he's leading your marriage and your family into a new place. Instead of the icy silence, now you're like newlyweds — all smoochy, smoochy — at your couples' Bible study group. Everybody else looks at each other and raises their eyebrows, whispering, "I don't understand it, but I can't deny it; you hated each other, and now you're making out during Bible study. I mean, something has happened!"

Maybe your teenage son or daughter was into all kinds of bad stuff, and now they've experienced an amazing turnaround through their relationship with Christ. All of a sudden they're going to youth group and leading a Bible study and playing in a praise band, and you're just in awe. You don't understand it, but there's no denying that a major change has happened.

Maybe you were addicted or you were in bondage or you were in fear, and something rose up inside of you and you're not the same. And other people looked on and said, "What happened? I can't understand it, but I won't deny it. Something's changed."

SPREAD THE WORD

The religious leaders confronted by Peter and John's healing in the name of Jesus couldn't deny it, and they didn't know what to do with it. But they did know that it would be a disaster if this kind of thing spread. They said, "'To stop this thing from spreading any further among the people, we must warn them to speak no longer to anyone in this name.' Then they called them in again and commanded them not to speak or teach at all in the name of Jesus" (Acts 4:17 – 18).

Notice that these religious leaders wouldn't even say Jesus' name; they decided to warn Peter and John not to speak to anyone in "this name." The other notable point here is that they *commanded* them not to speak or teach about Jesus. It was understood that such a command from this group carried with it the threat of punishment — imprisonment at the very least. This wasn't a friendly suggestion: "I'll let you off with a warning but please don't speed again." No, this was a promise of pain if Peter and John kept on talking about Jesus.

But I'm sure you know there was no stopping these guys. "But Peter and John replied, 'Which is right in God's eyes: to listen to you, or to him? You be the judges! As for us, we cannot help speaking about what we have seen and heard'" (Acts 4:19 – 20). Because they believed deeply, they were going to have to speak boldly. The two words in the Greek translated here as "cannot help" basically mean "it's not possible."

This phrase conveyed a sense of conviction every bit as firm and powerful as the Jewish leaders' command. Basically, Peter and John said, "You need to understand, you can threaten us, but we're still speaking. You can beat us, but we'll speak louder. You can put us to death, but the last words we're going to speak will be the name of Jesus, because if you've seen what we've seen and if you've heard what we've heard, you've just got to tell it. It's that good! If you saw the people that we were and the people that we are now, if you saw the sins he's forgiven, you'd have to talk about it. If you saw the miracles we've seen, you wouldn't be able to keep it to yourself."

When you're excited about something, you talk about it. When you see a great movie, you want to tell your friends to go see it. If it was a guy movie, you tell them, "Yeah, and all the trucks blew up before the big shootout. It was awesome! You've got to see it." Or if it's a chick flick and you're telling your chick-flick-loving friend about it, you say, "You've got to see it. It's just so romantic! He walked in the room and said, 'You had me at hello.'"

If you go to a restaurant and have an incredible meal and amazing service, then you can't wait to tell others how great your experience was. You want them to go there and enjoy the same kind of experience. When you hear a great new song on the radio, you want your friends or your spouse or kids to hear it. Unless it's a Justin Bieber song, and then you change the station. (Just joking. After watching *Never Say Never*, now I'm a Belieber.)

When you experience something so powerful, so life-changing as the love of God and the gift of Christ, then you're compelled to tell others about it. And no authority on earth can prevent you from speaking bold words of truth for all to hear.

TALKING TO YOURSELF

You might not feel bold with words. Your insecurities keep you quiet, timid, and reserved. But as you get to know Christ and you become who you are supposed to be, you simply can't hold back. I believe there are four areas in which God wants you to speak your witness and not just live it. These are areas in which you speak boldly because you believe so deeply and trust so firmly. The first one is this: because I believe so deeply, there are times I must speak boldly to myself.

This is what David did, as we see in 1 Samuel 30:6. David was greatly distressed because the people spoke of stoning him, so he encouraged himself in the Lord his God. I love this — he just preached himself a sermon! He strengthened his faith by reminding himself of the truth. He spoke boldly to himself.

> Because I believe so deeply, there are times I must speak boldly to myself.

We don't know what he said. Maybe he said, "I just remember the time when God gave me the strength to kill the lion, and the tiger, and the bear, oh my!" Or he might have said, "I remember when God gave me the faith to stand down the giant when everyone else said he was too big to beat. I said he was too big to miss and took him out!" Perhaps he said, "I've been through tough things before, and God protected me and saw me through them."

When we tell ourselves the truth, both from God's Word and from events in our lives when God's intervention was undeniable, we use the power of bold words to boost our faith. I've got a friend who battled with lustful thoughts for decades and couldn't overcome the problem. Then he started preaching to himself every day. Telling himself the truth about who he was, who God is, and who women are helped him to break a stronghold. God's Word renewed his mind, and suddenly he woke up and said, "I'm no longer battling with lust." What did he do? He preached his way boldly to victory in his life.

You can do the same thing. If you've never preached a sermon to yourself, it's time you tried. The next time you're overwhelmed with too much to do, just say, "Yes, I've got babies everywhere, diapers and dishes and domestic duties, but I can do all things through Christ who gives me strength." If you're overwhelmed at your business, with too much to do and not enough time to do it all, just say, "When I am weak, he is strong. It's not by my power or by my might, but it's by his Spirit, says the Lord."

When you're afraid, you just preach to yourself, "God has given me a spirit not of fear but of power and of love and of a sound mind." When you're worried, you just preach God's Word to yourself. "I will not be anxious about anything, but in everything by prayer and petition, I will submit my request to God, and I will let the peace of God, which supersedes all my understanding, guard my heart and my soul in Christ Jesus."

Because you believe so deeply, you have the power to give yourself bold encouragement by reminding yourself of God's truth.

TWO BIRDS WITH ONE PRAYER

The second area of speaking boldly moves us from ourselves to others: because I believe so deeply, I can't help but encourage you. I believe with all of my heart that the body of Christ, we as Christians, should be the most encouraging people on planet earth. Scripture couldn't be clearer about this principle: "Encourage one another daily" (Heb. 3:13). Every single day, as long as it's called a day, you should be encouraging others using God's Word.

You never know how your encouragement may change someone's life. Years ago, back when I was an associate pastor in a Methodist church, I was in charge of single adults' ministry, and it hadn't been going so well. I was so loud and aggressive about promoting singles' events at church that some members went before our board and said, "Craig's out of control. He should be fired for trying to turn our church into nothing but a singles' club."

> Because I believe so deeply, I can't help but encourage you.

At the time, I was just trying to get someone to show up. But as I look back on it now, I think they were right in asking me to dial it down. Because I had been so aggressive in promoting our singles' ministry, the church board forbade me from making any announcements during our worship services. However, one Sunday I was assigned the pastoral prayer during the service and thought I could kill two birds with one prayer, so to speak.

"Dear God in heaven," I stood in my robe and prayed, "I thank you that on this Friday night at 7:00 p.m., the single adults from around the city will come to our church at the east door, and that they will all, oh God, bring ten dollars to cover their pizza and their bowling. I pray in the name of Jesus that they would sign up on their communication card to drop off any kids in child care, and, God, I thank you that we're going to see revival this Friday night at 7:00 p.m., at the east door, as single adults from all over the city descend on this place. In the name of Jesus, amen."

Yes, I probably should have been fired, because I really did that! When my prayer hit the fan, and board members were saying, "Craig, we're not sure if you can keep working here," I was more than discouraged. I went home and told Amy, "Maybe I should just quit. Maybe I'm not good enough. Maybe I missed this whole God thing."

I never will forget what happened next. Amy looked at me and she spoke boldly God's Word: "Do not grow weary in doing good. For at the proper time you will reap a harvest if you do not give up! Craig Groeschel, I didn't marry a quitter; I married a finisher! And you will finish what God called you to do."

And I'm still in ministry today because someone encouraged me to keep on going. And I want to encourage you, because the same is true for you. Don't quit. Don't grow weary in doing good, for at the proper time and in the proper season, you will reap a harvest if you do not give up. Don't give up on your marriage. Don't give up on your dream. Don't give up on the vision that God has given you. Don't give up on the ministry that you know is buried deep within your heart. And by all means, do not give up on God, because God will never give up on you.

YOU STAND CORRECTED

The third area in which God calls us to speak boldly is perhaps the most challenging: because I believe so deeply, I can't help but lovingly correct you. Please notice that I said "lovingly." I'm not talking about using God's Word or his standards as license to judge others and be a jerk. Don't make up a huge "You're Going to Hell!" sign and think that you're lovingly correcting others. That's not bold; it's stupid.

Don't go home and be one of those jerk husbands who takes out his Bible as a sword and cuts his wife with it: "Be quiet, woman! You shouldn't speak; you just submit to me!" No, that's abuse; that's not biblical correction. When someone steps outside of the Word of God and you love them too much to let them stay there, then you're called to confront them with the truth in love. Don't be one of those jerk wives who nags her husband to be a better spiritual leader and then criticizes every move he makes with a Bible verse on top.

> Because I believe so deeply, I can't help but lovingly correct you.

No, when you correct someone in love, you make it clear that you're not better than they are. You make it clear that you truly do love them and that it's your love that's motivating you, not your self-righteous ego. You want the best for your brothers and sisters in

Christ, and to remain silent while they're drifting away from God amounts to keeping quiet when there's a snake underfoot.

Maybe your best friend is always trash talking her husband. "He's not a spiritual leader, he never initiates anything, blah, blah, blah." Maybe you need to say, "You know what? I love you and I care about your marriage too much to let you keep talking him out of who God wants him to be. He will never become the man of God that God wants him to be when you continue to cut him off at the knees. I know you well enough to know that you want to speak life, to speak love, to speak encouragement, and I'm not going to let you talk trash any longer. I love you too much to let you tear him down."

It could be that everyone in your circle of friends knows that one of you is addicted — to drugs, to alcohol, to pornography, to work — and yet no one has the spiritual fortitude to look this person in the eye and tell them the truth. But because you love this person too much to abandon them to their addiction, you are going to lovingly tell them the truth about their addictive behavior. You are going to stand in their way and say, "I'm here not as someone who is better than you but as someone who loves you. I'm not going to let you spiral down; I'm going to help you get help. I'm going to stand by you, and together we are going to kick this addiction. I love you too much to let you hurt yourself."

It could be one of your buddies is leaving his wife to chase some young skirt, and you know what you must do if you care anything about him at all. You're going to get in his face, because no one else will, and you're going to say, "Hey, I'm going to be the best friend you've ever had, and you may want to hit me and hate me, and that's fine. But I was there the day you said 'I do' before God and promised to love your wife as faithfully as Christ loves the church. I'm not going to let you play with this poisonous snake of temptation, because Satan is a liar, and what you're chasing will destroy your life. Get your butt back home, be a man of God, love your bride, and be a dad to your kids. You're not going to let some other man raise your kids, and neither am I. I love you too much."

Bold words, I know. And why would you say any of these things? Not because you're better but because you believe deeply. And when you believe deeply, you've got to speak boldly.

BOLD RUNS DEEP

The fourth area in which God invites us to speak boldly may be my favorite one: because I believe so deeply, I can't help but lead you toward Christ.

"I can't help it." This is what the disciples said. You can beat us, you can lock us up, you can threaten to kill us, but we cannot help speaking about what we've seen and heard. We can't help it, we're just going to do it, and you can't talk us out of it. It's never, ever going away. It's part of who I am at the deepest level of my being. I cannot *not* tell you about the one who means the most to me.

> Because I believe so deeply, I can't help but lead you toward Christ.

Other pastors often ask me, "Craig, do you always, every time you preach, week after week, invite people to turn from their sins and follow Christ?" And my response is always the same, "Abso-freakin-lutely! I do it, every single time, every single week." Why? Because I grew up in a church but didn't understand the essence of the gospel. I had head knowledge of God, but not a heart relationship with God.

And here's what you need to understand. When you've seen what I've seen, and when you've heard what I've heard, you can't be quiet about it. If you just knew who I was, how much filth I've been in, and if you had any idea what God has forgiven me of, and how much he's transformed me from an angry, bitter, unfaithful, lying person into, by his grace only, a man of God, then you'd realize that I have to talk about this God, this Jesus, this love that has radically changed my life.

To ask me to remain silent about the most important part of my life — why, you might as well ask the sun to stop shining or the birds to stop singing, the rain to stop falling or the flowers to stop bloom-ing. As long as there's breath in my body, nothing will stop me from talking about the Jesus who saved me and made me new.

Here's the deal, if you don't speak boldly, maybe it's because you don't believe deeply. Because when you believe deeply, I'm telling you, you can't live for the lower things of the world. You can't be like the world-followers selling out to material things. There's something in you; you've got to make a difference.

You're not going to rely on your actions alone to be your wit-ness about the one you love the most. Sometimes there's such a great opportunity that you can't keep it to yourself; you've just got to say who he is, what he's done. You cannot stop talking about what you've seen. You speak boldly about what you believe deeply.

chapter 12

bold obedience

There is no justification without sanctification,
no forgiveness without renewal of life,
no real faith from which the fruits
of new obedience do not grow.

— Martin Luther

When I was a new Christian, twenty years old and still in college, I went to church one Sunday and received an unexpected economics lesson. I was worshiping and singing and happened to look across the aisle a few rows up when I noticed a certain lady there at the end of the pew. She looked older, or maybe just weary and tired, and I sensed that she was having a tough time. By the end of worship, God had given me a burden for her, so I prayed for her several times. Then I felt like God told me, "Give her all the money you have in your wallet."

Now, I'd never had anything like this happen before, so I wondered, "Is that really God or just the supreme pizza I ate at 2:00 a.m. kicking in?" Then I thought, "Maybe it's Satan. Wait a minute. Why would he tempt me to be generous to a total stranger?" As my mind attempted to process something that was supernatural in origin, I finally said, "Okay, I'll give her the money, but how much do I even have?" Looking in my wallet, I saw a five-dollar bill, and was both relieved as well as annoyed. "That's stupid! How much good is five bucks going to do her?" At the same time, I was a college student, and five bucks was my next meal.

I kept wrestling with the sense that God wanted me to do this, but it didn't go away. So finally, I went up to her and said, "Excuse me — ma'am? I'm sorry, I know this is kind of odd, and it's not much, but it's all I have, and I felt like I was supposed to give you this." I handed her the five-dollar bill. Would she be offended? Annoyed? Insulted?

She just stood there for a moment looking at the money in her hand, and then she looked at me, and finally she threw her hands up and said, "Thank you, God!"

I thought, "Is she mocking me? What's the deal? Did God just multiply it in her hand and change Abe Lincoln's picture to Ben Franklin's? What's going on?" I started to walk away, embarrassed by how awkward I felt about my attempt at irrational obedience.

Before I could take more than two steps, the woman grabbed me and said, "No, wait! You have to hear this!" Through tears, she said, "I'm a single mom and I'm out of money, and I don't get paid until next Wednesday. When I looked at the fuel gauge in my car today, I wanted to go to church but had only enough gas to get here and not enough to get home. So I prayed, 'God, what do I do?' And I felt like God said, 'Go to church and trust me to get you home.' And God has answered my prayer and met my need. Thank you!"

"Wow! That's just, that's incredible!" I said and walked away smiling. As I headed toward the church parking lot, a guy I knew came up and said, "Hey, you want to go to lunch?"

I shook my head. "No, sorry—I can't." My lunch money was now someone else's gas money. But it was okay.

My buddy grinned. "I'm buying!"

"I'm there, baby!" I said.

And that's how I got an eight-dollar lunch from a five-dollar gift. No, that wasn't my goal, but I believe this is how God often works. When you obey him and bless someone, then he'll often use someone else's blessing to overflow and bless you. I believe Christians often perceive obedience to God as some test designed just to see if we're really committed to him. But what if it's designed as God's way of giving us what's best for us?

ROOTED IN LOVE

Some Christians seem to view obedience as this ball and chain that keeps them from doing all the things that they'd really like to do. Instead, I believe true obedience overflows from our passion for God, lovingly yielding our decision-making process to him. Obedience is not a matter of going through the motions and just doing the right thing; that's legalism and heartless participation in a merit system. That's living with our egos in charge, trying to earn God's favor so we can feel smugly self-righteous about ourselves.

Bold obedience is rooted in love and allows us to experience God's presence in a new and very real way. Like any relationship, it's about communication and cooperation. God consistently speaks to us and asks us to respond to the promptings of his Spirit and the teachings in his Word. This is living from our altar egos, sacrificing all that we're tempted to cling to in order to embrace all that God has for us.

We see this in the early Christian church, those small communities of believers meeting in people's homes and in secret locations. You'll recall in the last few chapters that we've seen Peter and John and these followers of Jesus do some pretty bold things, despite ongoing opposition.

First, they were preaching all about Christ, even though it's clear that the Jewish leaders, the Sanhedrin, didn't want to hear anything having to do with the so-called resurrection of their troublemaking nemesis, Jesus. But this didn't deter Peter and John a bit. They healed a lame man, who'd been crippled for forty years, in the name of Jesus, and this really freaked out the religious leaders.

Now the leaders were in a bind because everybody knew that the guy who was lame was now healed. Consequently, Christianity spread as the disciples preached boldly, cast out demons, and prayed to God for miracles. The Sanhedrin felt the pressure to shut it down before it got out of hand, if it hadn't gotten out of hand already.

Not surprisingly, the Bible explains that these leaders became jealous of the disciples. "Then the high priest and all his associates, who were members of the party of the Sadducees, were filled with jealousy. They arrested the apostles and put them in the public jail. But during the night an angel of the Lord opened the doors of the jail and brought them out. 'Go, stand in the temple courts,' he said, 'and tell the people all about this new life'" (Acts 5:17–20).

AGAINST THE GRAIN

From the experience of these early Christians, we can see three principles regarding the consequences of bold obedience. The first may seem obvious, but often prevents many of us from giving one hundred percent to obeying God: bold obedience usually triggers opposition. Despite the fact that Peter and John and company already had been arrested once before by these upset leaders, they continued to do what God asked them to do — preach and teach about Jesus in public. It should be no surprise that this landed them behind bars again.

Many Christians today believe their obedience is a down payment on God's reward program. They think that if they're obedient to God, he "owes" them elite, frequent-prayer, gold-miles status with no painful or challenging times. And I confess, I've been guilty of this mindset myself.

For example, a while back when I was late driving to church, I drove a little over the speed limit trying to make up for lost time. When I looked in the rearview mirror and saw the flashing blue lights, I quickly prayed, "God, please

> **Bold obedience usually triggers opposition.**

allow me to talk him out of giving me that ticket, because I am your faithful servant on my way to preach. In Jesus' name I pray." It's funny now, but I'm still a little embarrassed as I compare a speeding ticket with the kinds of persecution the early Christians experienced, as well as things that so many believers around the world experience today.

Have you had this kind of spiritually entitled thought? "I'm obeying God, so I should be married to a smoking-hot wife who loves the

Bible." Or, "I'm obeying God most of the time, so our kids should never get sick." And, "I should get an A on my algebra exam because I read my Bible today." And, "My football team should go undefeated this year because I'm a strong Christian." And, "I've worked hard and been obedient to God, so I should get a refund on my taxes this year."

Sounds a little like, "Santa, I've been such a good kid this year, so you'd better bring me what I'm asking for." The reality is that when we boldly obey God, we will face opposition. Bold obedience is not for wimps. If you're not ready to face opposition for your obedience, you're not ready to be used by God. When you obey God, opposition comes. Instead of smooth sailing, you may have to swim upstream in choppy water. Instead of gliding along, you may have to go against the grain.

In my life, let me tell you, every time — *every single time* — that God has used my obedience in a significant way to advance his kingdom, there's been major opposition.

When we started the church, I thought most Christians I knew would be like, "Oh praise God, young pastor boy's starting a new church! How can we pray for you?"

You know what I got? People looked at me like I said I was building an ark in the desert. "A church? Why are you starting a church? We've got plenty of churches. What's wrong with the church down the street? They're not good enough for you? Who do you think you are to go and start a new church when there's nothing wrong with the ones we already have?" Opposition.

As our church grew and we had to turn people away because of size limitations and fire codes, we became burdened to add another location (something that hadn't been done before to our knowledge).

"Church in another location? *Two* locations? What are you trying to do? Like, reach people for Christ? Come on, get real!" And then when we began utilizing technology: "That's crazy! That whole preacher-on-the-video-screen thing — who wants to watch a preacher on a video screen? Dumbest thing I've ever heard of."

And then when we started church online: "What? You can't have church online! Church is about people, not computers. That's ridiculous!" And then, we started giving the Bible away on mobile devices around the world. (Now averaging more than four million downloads per month.) Some people said, "You can't do that! The Bible is a book, not an app. You can't read the Word of God from your phone, for heaven's sake! It's got to have leather binding and gold-edged pages. Everybody knows that."

Every significant act of obedience faced tremendous opposition. So if you want to boldly obey God, then just put it down on your calendar — opposition is coming! But don't worry when you meet opposition for obeying God. Worry when you don't have opposition, because you're probably not obeying God.

I don't know what it will be for you. You could be sick and tired of debt, and you finally hear God asking you to make your finances a priority, and you say, "I'm sick of it. I don't want a financial noose around my neck. We're getting out of debt." As you pray about it, God might lead you to do something crazy. You might end up driving an old clunker instead of leasing or borrowing for a new car. Maybe you'll end up downsizing into a smaller home, and everybody will say, "What are you doing? Don't do that! Stay with us. Stay in debt. That's what we do! Buy bigger. Buy more than you can afford. Borrow!"

If you obey God, you're going to get resistance. He may call you to do something countercultural in how you raise your kids. Maybe you don't put them in a sports league that plays on Sundays. God might prompt you to send a message to your children, as well as others, that the worship of God is more important than sports. "But if you don't put little Brittany in the traveling flag gymnast league now when she's five, how will she ever make the traveling flag gymnast Olympic team?" Without a doubt, you'll get opposition when you follow God's path.

Maybe you're single and you've started to feel like a jerk magnet — every guy you date turns out to be one. So instead of feeling frantic to find a boyfriend and depressed by all the jerks you encounter, you feel God asking you to just enjoy being alone with him for a while. Then when your friends call and want you to meet them at the bar, they're not going to understand. "What? Are you becoming a nun or something? Come on, it's only one drink! Lots of hot guys will be there!" I'm telling you, when you obey God, you will see opposition. Don't worry when you do; worry when you don't.

> **When you obey, you can expect God to show up and work supernaturally.**

OUR GOD RAINS

Yes, you can expect opposition when you boldly obey God, but you can also expect him to show up in amazing ways. When you boldly obey, he will surprise you with solutions and answers and provision where it appears impossible. The second major principle we see from the early Christians is that when you boldly obey, you often release God's miracles. When you obey, you can expect God to show up and work supernaturally.

And it's often without a lot of fanfare. I love the way Luke, the writer of Acts, reports the big angelic jailbreak: "But during the night an angel of the Lord opened the doors of the jail and brought them out" (Acts 5:19). No big exciting buildup, no emotional embellishment, no dramatic spin. Just matter-of-fact, here's-what-happened-folks style of reporting. Just a statement.

Now, let's be honest. If you or I saw an angel, let alone one who came to bust us out of the big house, we'd be way over the top: "You're not going to freakin' believe this! This angel, who was, like, nine feet tall, had these flowing blinding-white robes. And this whooshing sound like wind rushing. And he had this *huge* sword that you could kill an elephant with. Well, he came in ..." and on and on we'd go. We'd be hanging around the jail cell with our jaws on the floor, begging, "Can I get a picture with you, Mr. Angel?" And you know we'd be live-tweeting it.

Why didn't Luke give us a big, show-stopping description? Because when you obey God, you're not surprised by the miracles of God. When you walk in the obedience of God, you're not surprised when he shows up and does something supernaturally. Keep in mind that it's not the "Lord, you owe me" mindset we were just talking about. They were in jail, after all. But in the middle of a bad situation, God sent an angel to free them.

When we walk in the obedience of God, we shouldn't be surprised when God comes through. We shouldn't be, but we often are. I've shared several of the crazy-miraculous events I've been privileged to experience. But I still find myself surprised when God does something cool. Recently, after hearing me preach about praying bold prayers, my son Sam, who's twelve, said, "Dad, let's boldly ask God to make it rain."

Now, realize that at the time, we were experiencing one of the most scorching summers on record for the state of Oklahoma. We'd gone fifty consecutive days with temperatures reaching over 100 degrees, even as high as 112. It seemed like it hadn't rained since 2003. And here's my son, getting all excited, saying, "We just need to ask God for some rain," as if he were the first to think of the idea.

So I nodded at Sam and pulled out my phone and opened the weather app. The ten-day forecast showed zero percent chance of rain, with sweltering heat. I tried to hedge. "Hey Sambo, that's a real bold prayer! But you know God knows best, and he may not be in the mood to make it rain just yet."

Sam said, "Dad! You said pray *boldly*."

Busted. So I said, "Yeah, yeah, yeah, okay, okay, I know, but let's just kind of pray for rain and some other things too." We prayed together, and at the end, Sam said, "God, I know it's not supposed to, but I just believe you can make it rain." This was on Sunday.

The next day, Monday, I'm sitting in my office, and I hear this rumbling sound that's vaguely familiar. At first, I thought it was just a jet flying lower than normal, but then the rumbling got louder and sounded like that crazy thing I remembered called thunder. I darted outside, and sure enough, a storm was brewing. As I looked up, large liquid drops like glass marbles began falling from the sky. I laughed and shouted, "Rain, baby, rain!"

I ran back inside and called Sam. "Hey, look outside — it's raining!"

He said, "Duh, Dad — we asked God to do it!"

PRICELESS FAITH

The third important lesson that emerges from the disciples' experience is that bold obedience always requires faith. Without faith, it's impossible to please God. Every single time he prompts you to do something, it's going to take faith to obey him.

Where do we begin? For me, the starting line is obeying God's Word. The Bible says that God's Word is a lamp unto our feet. What does that mean? If it's a light shining on our feet, we may be able to see the next step, maybe two, but not five and not twenty, because it's a lamp to our feet, not a spotlight on our future. If we obey step-by-step, then guess what? The lamp gives us the next step or two, and as we obey, God continues to reveal and we obey him one step at a time. We do the next thing and then the next, aware that we may not know where we're going exactly or where we'll end up. Only that God will lead us.

> Bold obedience always requires faith.

Recently, I entered into one of the biggest faith chapters in my life. After fasting for twenty-one days, seeking God for his direction for our church, I became burdened that he wanted us to reach more people by building five new church buildings. Now, in case you don't know, the last thing that excites me about ministry is building huge structures, elaborate campuses, and mega-offices. The body of Christ has bones, not bricks.

But I also know that buildings provide good places for the church to gather, to learn, and to grow. So I came up with a bold plan and described it to our church. The short version is that we'd build two permanent buildings for campuses that had been meeting in schools. We'd start two brand-new campuses in new cities. And we'd add a kids' building at another location. And here was the clincher: "And we're going to do these five buildings, which God has put on my heart, and pay for all of them with cash!"

Everyone at church seemed excited but was practical enough to wonder the obvious, multi-million-dollar question: "How are we going to do that?"

I said, "Honestly, I haven't figured out how, but I believe God will make it happen."

When I came home from church, Amy said, "You've never done anything like that before! That was bold!" She paused and asked, "How much is that all going to cost?"

"I have no idea yet," I said. "I haven't even thought about how to add it all up."

Amy said, "You're Planner Boy! You'd better get busy and figure out how much it will cost."

So I did. With pencil and paper in hand, I started thinking, "This building, okay about that many million. And this one ... plus ... equals ... carry five. And then the other one, well, okay, about that much ... and then ... oh, wow!" The bottom-line number, I'm telling you, was beyond impossible. Based on everything I knew, physically and literally and financially, it was impossible.

Naturally, I began to second-guess myself. I could just see it. After fifteen good years with my integrity intact, the church members were going to take me out behind our building and stone me with cement blocks for being a false prophet. This kind of goal was insane. My doubt began to devour my conviction.

As I've said before, though, God delights in using unlikely people to do impossible things for his kingdom. Relying on him and his grace and his provision, I'm here to tell you God did it. He empowered us to pay cash for all of the buildings in one year with no fundraisers, pledges, car washes, or bake sales. God is just that good!

With God, all things are possible. When you boldly obey, you will face opposition, and it will take faith, and your faith often will be met with God's miracles.

As you're reading, God might be leading you to start a small group in your home. And you're thinking, "How?" It's going to take faith.

Or you might feel compelled to start a ministry or a business or a new direction for your family than the one you've been on. Or you may be a single person, and you're feeling God compel you to ask that really cute other single person from your new small group out for coffee. And maybe you're going to develop a friendship, and God is going to spark the relationship, and the next thing you know, you're married and planning to name your first son "Craig." (After that crazy guy who got the ball rolling by challenging you to obey God and live by faith.)

Listen for God's voice. Live by faith. Learn to expect the unexpected.

LIFE SAVERS

Whenever God prompts you, you obey completely and you obey immediately no matter what. Bold obedience doesn't wait or waffle. After the angel freed the disciples from jail, we're told, "At daybreak they entered the temple courts, as they had been told, and began to teach the people" (Acts 5:21).

Don't you love it? At daybreak! Notice what they didn't do: they didn't delay; they didn't think about it and pray some more and decide to have a big breakfast at Denny's and mosey over to the temple courts after finishing their coffee. They obeyed fully and promptly. We must realize that true obedience is total and timely. Delayed obedience is disobedience. Partial obedience is disobedience.

If it's big, you obey. If it seems small and insignificant, you still obey. What seems minor and trivial to us may in fact be a big deal in the scope of what God's up to. This really came home to me recently when Amy and I were in Hawaii. I was teaching a leadership event there (someone has to sacrifice and help those people learn about God) and had filled up the four days with virtually no time for the two of us to relax and enjoy the beauty of the islands.

Finally, my responsibilities were over, and Amy and I strolled down to the beach to unwind. We'd been there about thirty seconds when suddenly God gave me a burden for a friend of mine who I knew was going through a rough time. After another few minutes, I said, "Amy, I'm really sorry; I know it's been an all-ministry week, but I think I'm supposed to call this guy."

She said, "You think God wants you to?"

I said, "Yes."

She said, "What're you waiting on? Call him!"

So I dialed his number and immediately realized that I'd forgotten about the difference in time zones; it would be almost midnight where he was. After a few rings, my friend picked up and said, "Why are you calling me now?"

> Delayed obedience is disobedience. Partial obedience is disobedience.

I apologized. "Sorry I forgot about the time difference. Just wanted to check in with you."

He paused and said, "Why now?" and his voice sounded shaky and nervous.

"I told you, I just felt like catching up. I'm sorry it's late, but I felt like — "

And he said, "No! Why *now*?"

"Well, honestly, God just really put you on my heart." And then it dawned on me. I said soberly, "You're thinking about taking your life right now, aren't you?"

Silence. Then he said softly, "Yes."

I said, "Do you have a gun with you?"

"Yes."

"Put the gun down, because it's obvious God cares for you enough to have me call you at the perfect time. You're going to walk out your door, go to your neighbor's house — I don't care what time it is — ring the doorbell, and you're staying the night there. Agreed?"

He hesitated, and I said, "Wouldn't you agree that God cares for you so much that he would have me call you at the right time?"

He said, "Yes, absolutely."

That was a couple of years ago, and my friend has worked through all of his issues and is so undeniably on fire for God now. Neither of us can deny God's direct involvement in saving and protecting his life, and in growing and deepening my faith. When we live by faith, the life we save may be our own. Not that we can save ourselves; only God can do that, of course. But we may discover who we really are and what it means to really live.

When God prompts you, even if it doesn't make sense, obey immediately and completely. We answer to a higher authority that may defy what seems logical, predictable, and normal from our human perspective. When Peter and John were once again brought before the Jewish leaders (a third time, if you're counting), they made their divine accountability undeniably clear. "We gave you strict orders not to teach in this name," they said. Peter responded, "We must obey God rather than huma beings!" (Acts 5:28 – 29).

We act boldly based on what we believe deeply. We obey boldly when we trust God completely. It's not an option, a subjective accessory to your faith; it's a main ingredient, must-have. When you fall so in love with God, you don't care what anybody else thinks, what anybody else says, how foolish it makes you look, or how weird it may seem by everyone else's standards.

If you want to move your ego out of the way and live by your altar ego, then you must be a servant of Christ. You know that no matter what others say, they can't stop you. They can threaten you, intimidate you, beat you, lock you up, but your faith will not waver. Why?

Because you must obey God rather than people. You're no longer who you thought you were. You are now who you were meant to be.

I pray that God will seal this truth deep within your heart. I hope that you'll embrace your true identity and live out of it. That your understanding of God will be different. That you'll see that when we spend time with God, it leads to faith, which leads to boldness, which leads to results, which leads to more desire for him, and more faith and more boldness and more glory to our Father.

Make us, oh God, in love with your Son, so much so that the world will be amazed by our boldness, and they will take note that we have been with Jesus.

final introduction

*Every new beginning comes
from some other beginning's end.*

— Seneca

It happened again about a month ago. Someone from college came to LifeChurch and stopped to talk to me after the service. With a look of uncertainty on her face, a woman about my age gasped slightly and said, "You're not ... You can't be ... There is no way you're the Craig Groeschel that I went to college with. He was the wildest guy on campus! You can't be him."

"Actually, you're right," I said, trying not to crack a smile. "I'm not *that* guy. That guy died years ago."

She looked taken aback, more than a little confused.

"That's right, almost twenty-four years ago," I explained, "I gave my life to Christ and the old Craig Groeschel died." The woman nodded, following my meaning. Like Paul said in Scripture, I told her, "I was crucified with Christ, yet I still live. But it is no longer the old Craig who lives, but now it is Christ who lives in me."

The woman smiled, clearly intrigued that I am and am not the

Craig Groeschel she knew all those years ago. As I've shared with you throughout this book, I don't have a split personality or an alter ego. Mine is an altar ego. My old life is on the altar, crucified with Christ. My new life is his. Christ in me. And the only reason I'm not still acting like I did in college is because of Jesus. I am not who I was. I am who God made me to be.

MIRROR IMAGE

If you'll remember, at the beginning of the book I confessed about the moment I looked into my own eyes in the mirror and finally admitted the painful truth. I didn't like the guy staring back at me. That guy was dishonest. He was selfish. And he was ungodly in every way. Somehow, the man in the mirror was simultaneously conceited and insecure. Popular and hated. Fun on the outside and miserable on the inside. Though I'd achieved and accomplished most of what I'd thought I wanted, I still missed what I truly needed.

Thankfully, in my pit of sin, God reached down and lifted me out through Christ. By the power of God's Word and the love of his Spirit, he made me into a new creation. He washed my sins away. I became new.

Sometimes God reminds me of who I used to be, like when an old friend from college comes up to me and says, "You can't be ..." And sometimes he gives me a dramatic glimpse of what I look like now. While I'm not perfect and won't be arriving there this side of heaven, I was recently stopped in my tracks by someone else's reflection of me.

At a recent meeting with the leaders from our church, my wife,

Amy, had asked to join us, which she does from time to time. I expected her to share her heart and do what she does so well: encourage, lift, and bless the people around her. After our meeting was underway, she asked if she could speak.

"Craig doesn't know I'm going to share this," Amy began and smiled, "but I want to tell you a little bit about the Craig you don't get to see."

Everyone laughed, including me, expecting her to tell some funny or embarrassing story about something I had done at home recently.

She waited for our laughter to subside and then said, "What you see from him when he preaches is only a glimpse of the man of God that he truly is." She paused to make the shift in mood very clear. "As the woman who's been married to him for more than twenty-one years, I want you to know that Craig is the most godly person that I know. He's humble. He's loyal. He's faithful. He's devoted. Craig is without a doubt a better husband to me and a daddy to our children than I could have even dreamed up in my wildest childhood hopes."

Tears welled up in my eyes. I tried to fight them back, act cool, and shake the powerful emotion, but nothing could stop my feelings from flowing out of my heart.

Amy continued and became choked with emotion herself. "I want you to know that Craig is fully devoted to Christ. Everything he does is for the glory of God. I can't believe that God allowed me to stand by the most faithful follower of Jesus that I've ever met."

And she was just getting started. Amy continued describing my character for almost ten minutes. I squirmed with embarrassment, overwhelmed, humbled, overjoyed, and amazed at her enormous gift.

I can't even describe it to you now without tearing up at the memory of all the things she said. Hearing that kind of spiritual affirmation from the one person in the world who knows me better than anyone else is hands down the most meaningful gift I could ever receive on this side of heaven.

COMMENCEMENT EXERCISE

I'll be as transparent as I know how to be. There's a big part of me that just loves, loves, loves that my wife feels that way about me. But there is an infinitely bigger part of me that has to stop and worship the God who changed me, knowing it is only because of him that any of what she said is true.

Let me encourage you to slow down your reading and get honest for a minute. If you've grown up around the church or been a Christian for a while, you know the lingo all too well: "I was saved." "Jesus changed my life." "I was lost, but now I'm found." "When I met Jesus, everything changed."

But I want to ask you to pause for a moment. Focus and read prayerfully. Let's reflect on some of the important ground we've covered together in this book.

If there's any part of your life that is not pleasing to God, God can change you. Is there any part of your life that's not pleasing to you? If you battle with insecurities, self-doubt, or spiritual inconsistencies, Christ can make you new.

Remember, because of Christ, you are not who others say you are. You are who God says you are. Who are you? Well, you're not your past. You're not what you did. You're not what others have done to you. You are an ambassador for Christ, God's representative sent from heaven to earth. You are God's masterpiece, created in Christ Jesus to do the good works God prepared in advance for you to do. You are an overcomer, by the blood of the Lamb and by the words of your testimony. You are a child of the living God and filled with the same Spirit that raised Christ from the dead.

You don't have to get caught up in your self-worth or lack thereof. Your worth is not based on your self. You are valuable because God says you are his.

I'm praying that God will use the words from this book to help you to sacrifice any old, unhealthy, untrue, and unbiblical thoughts about yourself. And that God will introduce you to your altar ego — who you are in Christ.

Because when you know who you are, you'll know what to do. Empowered by Christ in you, you can now live a life full of integrity. While others are constantly ungrateful, you'll be full of gratitude to your good God for all he's doing and for all he's done. Instead of seeking immediate gratification, you'll never trade the ultimate for the immediate. You'll wait for God's perfect will in his perfect time. And because of who he is, you'll give honor where honor is due. Not only will you show honor freely; you'll live honorably.

And as your confidence in your new Christ-esteem grows, so will your boldness. Because you know Christ, you'll pray bold prayers, speak bold words, and obey God boldly. You'll never be timid again. Because bold actions are born of bold beliefs.

So I'd like to introduce you to someone new. Just like God made me different, he'll do the same for you. By the power of the risen Christ in you, say goodbye to who you were and hello to who you can become. Let me introduce you to who you were meant to be.

Meet the new you!

You might have noticed that I called this last chapter a "Final Introduction." You have now been introduced to who you really are. You'll recall that in school, every time you finished one level, you had a commencement to the next. Which always seemed kind of strange to me as a kid because I was focused on middle school ending or on graduating from high school. But the word *commencement* means "beginning," and in life as in school, every time you graduate from one thing, you're moving on to something else. Once you conclude one thing, you're introduced to another.

Now that you know who you are, you'll know what to do. And whatever you do, do it all for the glory of the one who made you new.

acknowledgments

Thank you to all my friends who offered support, encouragement, and assistance with this book. I'm especially thankful for:

Dudley Delffs. You are the best of the best. I thank God for your editing partnership, but even more so for your friendship.

Tom Dean, Cindy Lambert, Brian Phipps, and the whole team at Zondervan. I'm eternally grateful for your Christ-centered heart for publishing.

Tom Winters. Thank you for believing in me and representing me well.

Brannon Golden. Nothing I write is complete without your contribution. Thanks for your faithfulness to our church, to Christ, and to me as a friend.

Lori Tapp. You always contribute way more than you know. Thanks for your loyalty, sacrifice, integrity, and faithfulness.

Catie, Mandy, Anna, Sam, Stephen, and Joy. I love watching you grow in your love for Christ. No dad is more proud of his kids than I am of you.

Amy. Thanks for supporting me and enduring all the challenges (and blessings) of ministry together. You are the love of my life. More than anything, I love your passion for Christ. I want to be more like you.

Altar Ego: A DVD Study

Becoming Who God Says You Are

Craig Groeschel

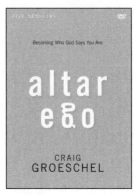

Most people are obsessed with the approval of others. The problem is that living for what people think of you is the quickest way to forget what God thinks about you.

In *Altar Ego*, a six-session DVD Bible study, pastor and bestselling author Craig Groeschel teaches that if there is any part of your life that is not pleasing to God, God can change it. If you battle with insecurities, self-doubt, or spiritual inconsistencies, Jesus can make you new.

You are not your past. You are not what you did. You are not who others say you are. You are who Christ says you are.

You don't have to get caught up in your self-worth or lack thereof. Your worth is not based on your opinion of yourself. You are valuable because God says you are his.

This DVD Bible study will help you sacrifice any old, unhealthy, untrue, and unbiblical thoughts about yourself and introduce you to your altar ego—who you are in Christ.

Available in stores and online!

ZONDERVAN®
.com

Soul Detox

Clean Living in a Contaminated World

Craig Groeschel

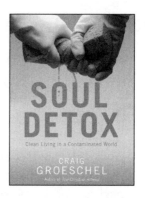

As standards of conduct continue to erode in our shock-proof world, we must fight the soul pollution threatening our health, our faith, and our witness to others. Without even knowing it, people willingly inhale secondhand toxins, poisoning their relationship with God and stunting their spiritual growth.

Soul Detox examines the toxins that assault us daily, including toxic influences, toxic emotions, and toxic behaviors.

By examining the toxins that assault us daily, this book offers the ultimate spiritual intervention with ways to remain clean, pure, and focused on the standard of God's holiness.

Available in stores and online!

Soul Detox: A DVD Study

Clean Living in a Contaminated World

Craig Groeschel

In *Soul Detox*, pastor and bestselling author Craig Groeschel sheds light on relationships, thoughts, and behaviors that quietly compromise our well-being. Through concise teaching and honest humor, Groeschel provides a source of inspiration and encouragement for a faith-filled lifestyle that will keep you free of spiritual toxins.

Our culture unknowingly ingests regular doses of spiritual toxins that assault our relationship with God. This five-session small-group DVD Bible study with participant's guide (sold separately) shines light on dark influences, emotions, and behaviors in order to empower Christians to live pure lives and grow closer to God.

Sessions include:

1. Lethal Language: Experiencing the Power of Life-Giving Words
2. Scare Pollution: Unlocking the Chokehold of Fear
3. Radioactive Relationships: Loving Unhealthy People without Getting Sick
4. Septic Thoughts: Overcoming Our False Beliefs
5. Germ Warfare: Cleansing Our Lives of Cultural Toxins

Soul Detox can be used in a variety of ways—as a whole church campaign (adult congregation), as an adult Sunday school study, as a small group study, or for individual Bible study. The DVD contains five 10 to 15 minute video teaching sessions from pastor Craig Groeschel, and the participant's guide provides individual and group activities, between-session personal studies, and additional background material that will enhance the experience of the video sessions.

WEIRD

Because Normal Isn't Working

Craig Groeschel,
author of The Christian Atheist

Normal people are stressed, overwhelmed, and exhausted. Many of their relationships are, at best, strained and, in most cases, just surviving. Even though we live in one of the most prosperous places on earth, normal is still living paycheck to paycheck and never getting ahead. In our oversexed world, lust, premarital sex, guilt, and shame are far more common than purity, virginity, and a healthy married sex life. And when it comes to God, the majority believe in him, but the teachings of Scripture rarely make it into their everyday lives.

Simply put, normal isn't working.

Groeschel's "weird" views will help you break free from the norm to lead a radically abnormal (and endlessly more fulfilling) life.

Available in stores and online!

ZONDERVAN®
.com

The Christian Atheist

Believing in God but Living as If He Doesn't Exist

Craig Groeschel

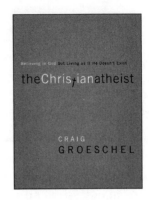

"The more I looked, the more I found Christian Atheists everywhere."

Former Christian Atheist Craig Groeschel knows his subject all too well. After over a decade of successful ministry, he had to make a painful admission: although he believed in God, he was leading his church as if God doesn't exist.

To Christians and non-Christians alike, to the churched and the unchurched, the journey leading up to Groeschel's admission and the journey that follows—from his family and his upbringing to the lackluster and even diametrically opposed expressions of faith he encountered—will look and sound like the story of their own lives.

Now the founding and senior pastor of the multicampus, pace-setting LifeChurch.tv, Groeschel's personal journey toward a more authentic God-honoring life is more relevant than ever.

Christians and Christian Atheists everywhere will be nodding their heads as they are challenged to honestly ask the question, Am I putting my whole faith in God but still living as if everything were up to me?

Available in stores and online!